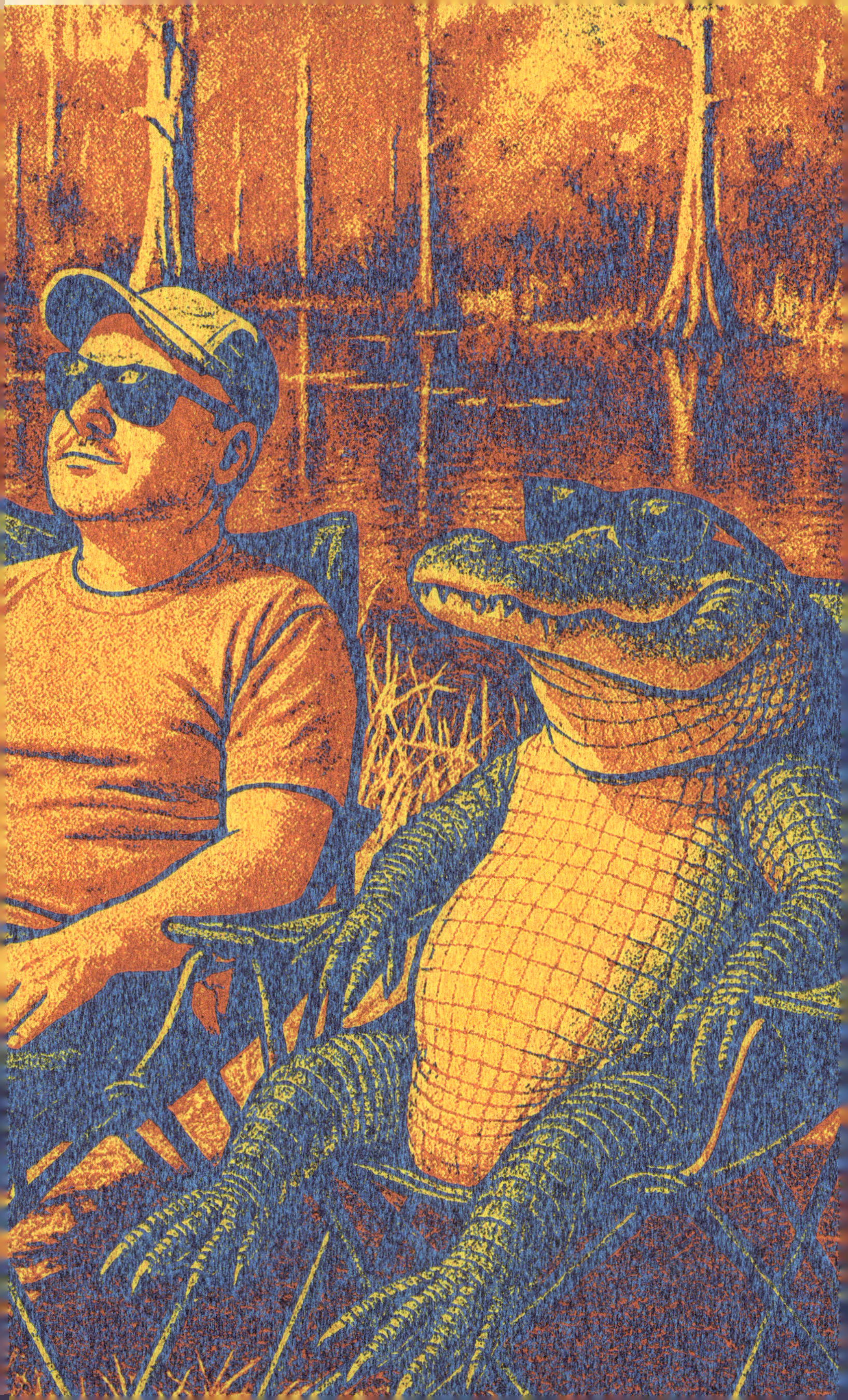

Afterword

WELL I'LL BE DARNED, YOU MADE IT TO THE END!

IF YOU'VE READ THIS FAR, *bless your heart*. Hopefully you've either recognized half these phrases from your own vocabulary, chuckled at the ones your parents or grandparents used to say, or furiously highlighted them for future anthropological research. Either way, thanks for coming along on this weird little linguistic road trip.

I wrote *For Pete's Sake*[2] because, honestly, I couldn't help but marvel at the way hearing someone say, "Don't make me turn this car around" can instantly summon the ghost of every sweaty summer road trip past in the family station wagon. How a simple "Look what the cat dragged in," takes me straight to green plastic bowls of noodle salads at 4th of July get togethers. Or how much "Heavens to Betsy" reminds me of the people who made me who I am. Sure, some of these expressions might be outdated. Some are confusing. Some are so deeply suburban they practically smell like freshly mowed lawn and boxed wine. But all of them carry a certain charm—one that's equal parts humor and *why the hell do we say that*?

It's about looking around—at ourselves, our families, our neighbors—and appreciating the strange beauty of how we talk to each other. How we connect. How we say "See ya later, alligator," eliciting an instinctual

"After a while, crocodile," and then bask in the warmth of neighborly affection.

So whether you're a lifelong practitioner of Caucasian Phraseology or just dipping your toes into the Aqua Velva-scented waters, I hope this book made you laugh, and provided a little insight into what makes this specific brand of speak so wonderfully uncool.

And remember:

If someone gives you trouble, tell 'em they're "Cruisin' for a bruisin'."

If all else fails, just scooch on out and say, "Let's blow this popsicle stand."

And most importantly, don't take any guff from a whippersnapper until you've had your coffee.

—Erin Tyler

PFLUGERVILLE, TEXAS
JUNE, 2025

---

2 No one knows who "Pete" is.

www.ingramcontent.com/pod-product-compliance
Lightning Source LLC
LaVergne TN
LVHW051939100826
845155LV00006B/17
* 9 7 9 8 8 9 8 1 4 5 3 1 6 *

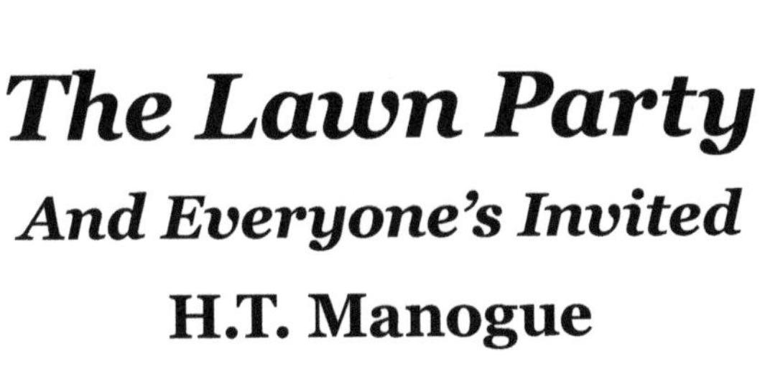

The Lawn Party

And Everyone's Invited

H.T. Manogue

The Lawn Party

Blades Of Grass You Get A Free Pass.

No Rules. No Pools.

Rocket Ride In A Natural Vibe.

Open That Thing That Wants To Sing.

Spacious Now. Nature Knows How.

Legions Of Ants Love To Dance.

Incarnate Signs Keep Flipping Time.

Perceptions Change In Searching Minds.

Engines Roaring. Planet's Boiling.

Foggy Room. Dreams In Bloom.

Say The Word

And Beliefs Build

A Herd.

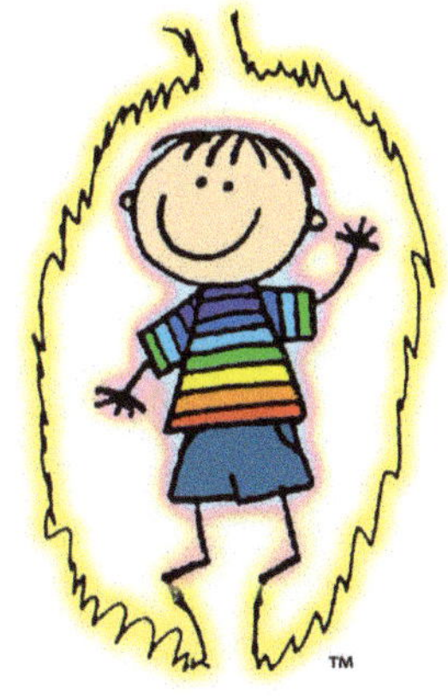

ISBN-13: 979-8-218-13700-7

Thelawnparty.net

www.shortsleeves.net

Other Works by H. T. Manogue

Poetry

Short Sleeves: A Book for Friends 2006 Children's Collection

Short Sleeves: A Book for Friends 2007 Children's Collection

Short Sleeves Spirit Songs 2008 Collection

Echoes From The Wind 2020 Collection

Novels

Living Behind the Beauty Shop
2011

The Butterfly Ball
2012

Bed Bosh & Beyond
2013–2014

Black Orchid Night
2015

Pine Cone Pandemic
2019

Just An Old Fashioned Love Song Meets Stoic Man
2021

Essays

Short Sleeves Insights: 2010 Collection – Out of Print

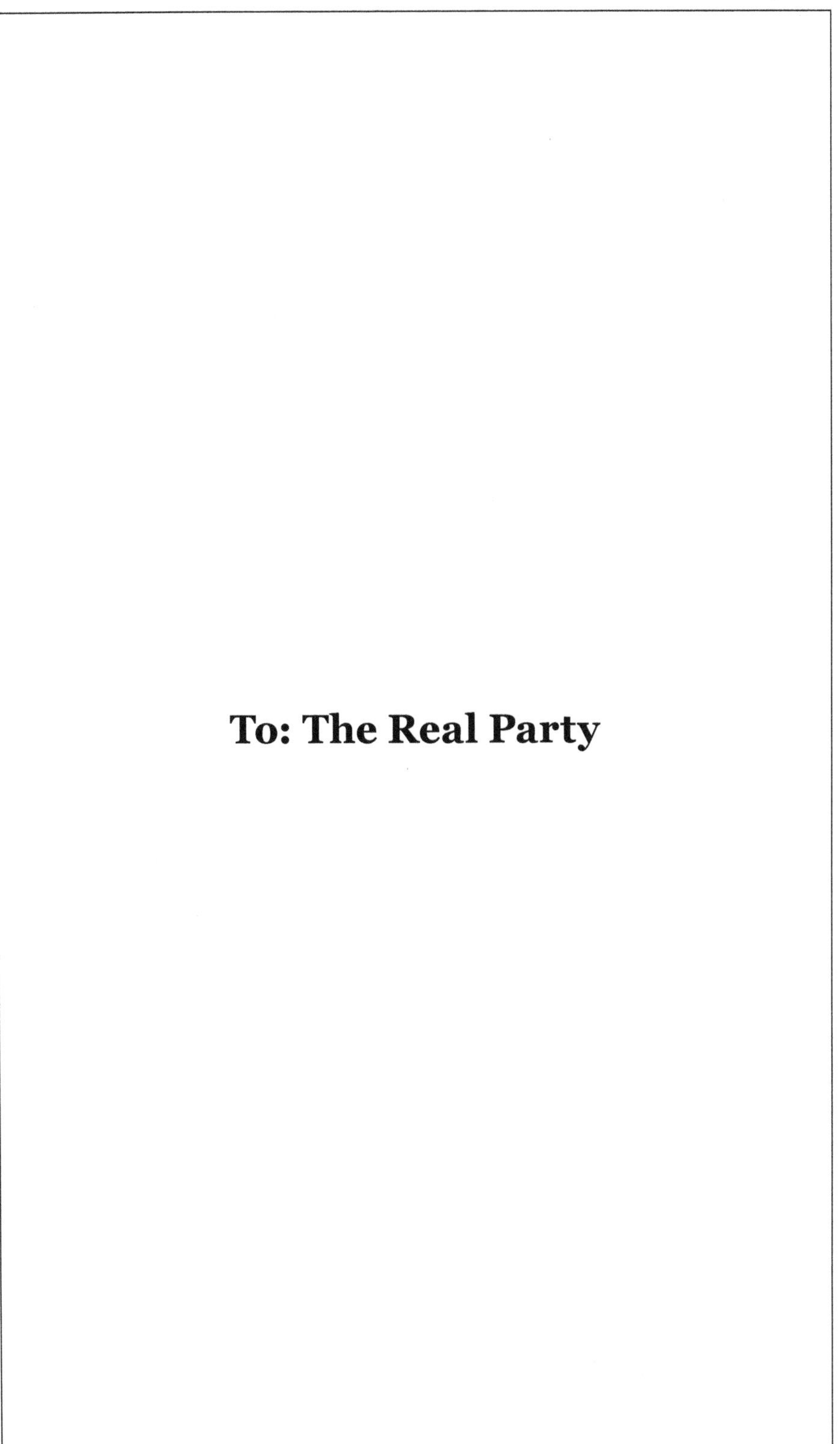

To: The Real Party

Paul Harmon Toast Revisited

An extrasensory feeling emerges when people spend a little time with Paul Harmon. Paul knows what he came here to do, and he does it in the true spirit of all creative artists. During one of the most creative times in the contemporary art scene, Paul had a studio in Paris and in Nashville.

Jean Michel Folon and other French and European artists recognized Paul's creations during his 10-year-painting extravaganza in Paris. Through the years, Jonathan Winters, Peter Max, and a list of celebrities, artists, politicians, and art lovers sat in awe as they listened to Paul discuss art, painting, and life in his Nashville studio.

Paul's art work sits in Monaco's Museum of Art and in the homes of European, American, and Asian art collectors. Few art lovers can resist Harmon's creations. His interpretation of the nuances in life inspire thoughts that light the imagination with the match of creative energy. Paul's sculptured faces and bodies have an ethereal aura about them.

Mr. Harmon's fine-tuned faces reveal the sensitivity in his work and the differences that exist within the diversity we create. But it's not just the faces and the bodies that show off Paul's creative genius. All his work has a touch of all of us in it. We get a chance to see what our reality looks like to Paul. And that may be one reason the Smithsonian asked Paul for some of his work. And the reason art lovers and museums around the world display his works of art.

Harmon's work can be a smorgasbord of landscapes, animals, bodies, and faces. The images, and all the subtle touches that create great art, explode in color-filled expressions on his canvases. Paul likes to add another dimension to his work by giving each piece a poetic title filled with aristocratic and abstract charm.

His never-ending trail of vibrant colors and dabs of inner energy, and his healthy dose of desire, make his work stand out in the art world. Paul has the innate ability to show there is more than one way to view the world. And many ways to accept it for what it is and is not. That seems to be the essence of the message in Paul's art. Harmon's art pings its way through different dimensions, and pongs our subjectivity with a deep connection that shakes us awake.

Paul decided to join me in my creative world six years ago. Four of my book covers are his creations. The books came together when Paul sat down in front of his giant Apple screen and did what he does so graciously on the days I visit his memory-filled studio. He created the front and back covers of those four books.

And he did it with a sense of excitement that is hard to put in words.

The beauty of knowing Paul does not just lie in his creations. His beauty lies in his rapturous southern gentleman charm and his one-of-a-kind personality. Paul weathered life's storms like a focused sea captain who appreciates his accomplishments and his challenges. Paul Harmon is his art, and his art is ours to cherish.

*****

Just An Old Fashioned Love Song Meets Stoic Man included this tribute to Paul. After Paul received his copy, he sent me his *About The 2021 Dedication.* Enjoy this piece of verbal artistry.

And get ready to experience a collection of paintings from Paul's 2021 *Her Face* collection. His thoughts and poems in the book display artistic talent at their finest.

As Paul notes in his own way somewhere in the book:

You don't have to understand my art.
Looking and reading are enough.

Visit Paul's website: **paulharmon.com**

About The 2021 Dedication

I thank my good friend Hal Manogue for his lofty, and yes, over the top praise of me and my work. I can only wish I were half that man and painter.

An important thing that Hal Manogue and I share is our mutual persistent search for the "true thing" in our art.

Some corrections are due. I cannot recall anyone being remotely awed by my story telling or art speak.

In fact, of those mentioned Jean Michel Folon was awed only by himself.

Jonathan Winters awed everyone in my studio with his wit and sweet humanity. I was one mouth agape in his audience.

As for Peter Max, I recall that we were both a bit drunk in our all-night musings on art and life.

Awe was not present in the room.

As to the Smithsonian, in 1955 the Archives of American Artists, Smithsonian Institute, asked to collect my papers and records.

I have sent bundles for about every decade since. That's the extent of their interest, for which I am so grateful.

Hal Manogue's heart is in the best of all places, and I love him for his unbridled exuberance.

Paul Harmon 2021

Front And Back Covers

Paul Harmon's front cover painting, *The Lawn Party*, hit me square between the eyes. Spending more than thirty years in the domestic and international shoe business, I was an easy mark.

The multicolored dress sandal reminded me of the shoes I helped source and sell from Brazil, China, and India. The engaging and present face threw my memory into wild shoe-dog motion. And I relived another time in my life: a time when a one-of-a-kind mind and an earring changed the direction of my life.

The Lawn Party represents a time of change in my life. The old days are memories now. But life's party continues in the words and thoughts in this book. Here's one:

Nothing Like A New Sandal
That Sinks In The Sand Of Poetry
And Smiles In The Contours
Of Its Own Beauty
HTM

The back cover is another Harmon creation. The damsel on the back is part of the 2021 *Her Face collection.* That painting opens a window that lets the colorful breeze of Harmon's art come alive.

Paul had to adjust the painting in order for it to fit the back cover. And those changes added another dimension to the book's character.

Trademarks

ACE

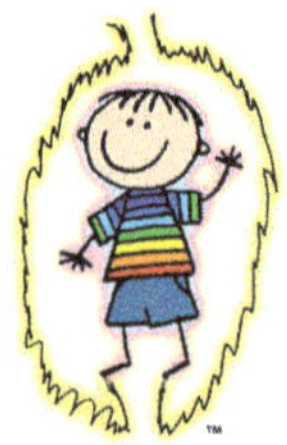

Aware Connected Energy

The Kids

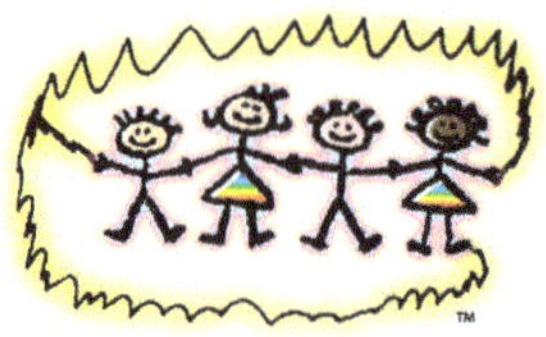

Freedom Awareness Connection & Contrast

Thank You:

Designer Jessica Galbraith

&

Lightning Source

Thanks To These Publishers For Their Artistic Contributions:

(All works available from your book source.)

HarperCollins Publishers Inc. And HarperSanFrancisco
The Essential Rumi Translated By Coleman Barks With John Moyne

Maypop Books, Athens, GA
Rumi, We Are Three: New Rumi Translations By Coleman Barks
Rumi—One-Handed Basket Weaving— Poems On The Theme Of Work Versions By Coleman Barks

Hohm Press, Prescott, AZ
Crazy As We Are — Mevlana Celaleddin Rumi Translations
By Dr. Nevit O. Ergin

Shambhala Publications, Inc., Boston, MA
The Teachings Of Rumi Andrew Harvey

Penguin Putnam Inc., New York, NY
The Glance— Songs of Soul-Meeting Translated By Coleman Barks
With Nevit Ergin

The University of Chicago Press, Chicago & London
Mystical Poems Of Rumi 1 First Selection, Poems 1-200

New Awareness Network Inc., Manhasset, NY
The Seth Material
Seth, Dreams And Projections of Consciousness
Seth Quotes By Jane Roberts and Robert F. Butts
© Laurel Davies

Amber-Allen Publishing Inc., San Rafael, CA
The Unknown Reality Volume One
The Unknown Reality Volume Two
Seth Speaks
The Way Toward Health
The Nature Of Personal Reality

Paul Harmon
Words on Art— Private Publication

Author's Notes

There's a mystical vibration surrounding this work—for a couple of reasons. First, the museum-quality artwork is in a league of its own. Second, the messages from the four poets transcend time and bounce off the walls of remembering.

Putting this book together, and contributing to the messages within it, opened another psychic avenue for me to travel.

Reading Rumi's 800-hundred-year-old thoughts again was a treat in itself. And then absorbing more thoughts from a non-physical personality called Seth brought me to an exhilarating bend in my awareness trail.

The underlying message in this book is a simple one. Our beliefs create our perceptions. And the choices from those perceptions become our experiences in some way.

The trick is identifying our intricate belief system. We have core beliefs about religion, science, sex, relationships, perception, the senses, duplicity, physical creation, emotion, and truth. And they help create our reality.

Mixed in with those core beliefs are beliefs we create through associations and influences. Those psychic messages color the various aspects of our core beliefs. So, sifting through a mental system that started before birth and continues as we age is a challenging task.

The messages in the book highlight our ability to choose what beliefs fit our personal truth. No one can change our current beliefs unless we choose to do so.

In the book,
Paul Harmon's verbal artistry brings clarity to his creative mission. With innate understanding, Harmon uses words to describe what he manifests physically. Harmon fans, and new friends, will come away knowing more about Paul Harmon and his value-fulfilling works of art after visiting The Lawn Party.

Seth drops a few hints about belief sifting. And Rumi lets us know our beliefs connect us no matter the language.

Cheers!

H.T.M
February 2023

A Little On Rumi

Jelaluddin Balkhi, born in Balkh, Afghanistan in 1207, became one of the Eastern world's respected spiritual teachers. In 1273, leaders from all religious sects attended his funeral.

His family fled to Konya, Turkey, between 1215 and 1220 to avoid the invading Mongol armies. In Turkey, his name changed to Rumi, which means *From Roman Anatolia.*

Rumi's collection of thoughts teaches unity instead of separation. His poems express love and compassion for all life.

More than 700 years after his physical death, Rumi is alive now, more than ever.

The 13th century was a different time. But Rumi's work has no time or measurement attached to it. His poems prove awareness and time intersect and become one in the knowing.

A Little About Seth

Jane Roberts, a woman living in Elmira, New York, in the 1970s, began interacting with a non-physical energy personality psychically who called himself Seth.

That interaction started more than fifty years ago. Jane, and her husband Robert Butts, wrote several books that include the thoughts of Seth.

Seth would speak using Jane's physical characteristics. But her characteristics and voice would slightly change when Seth had a psychic connection with Jane. Butts took notes of every meeting and put them in book form.

Seth continued to exchange information with Jane and Robert Butts until Roberts passed in 1984. The words in this book come from several Seth books.

Millions of people around the world believe the information provided by Seth on a plethora of different topics is hard to ignore. His non-physical thoughts give us a more comprehensive understanding of who we are—physically as well as non-physically.

Seth Quotes By Jane Roberts and Robert F. Butts

I always loved to paint and draw
But I didn't think
Of it as something
One did as a career.
It was an amusement,
But I did identify Myself
With It Early On.

Paul Harmon

When you are in touch with your psyche,
You experience direct knowledge.
Direct knowledge is comprehension.
When you are dreaming,
You are experiencing direct knowledge
about yourself or about the world.
You are comprehending
Your own being
In a different way.

Seth

Listen To The Presences
Inside Poems
Let Them Take You
Where They Will
Follow Those Private Hints
And Never Leave
The Premises

Rumi

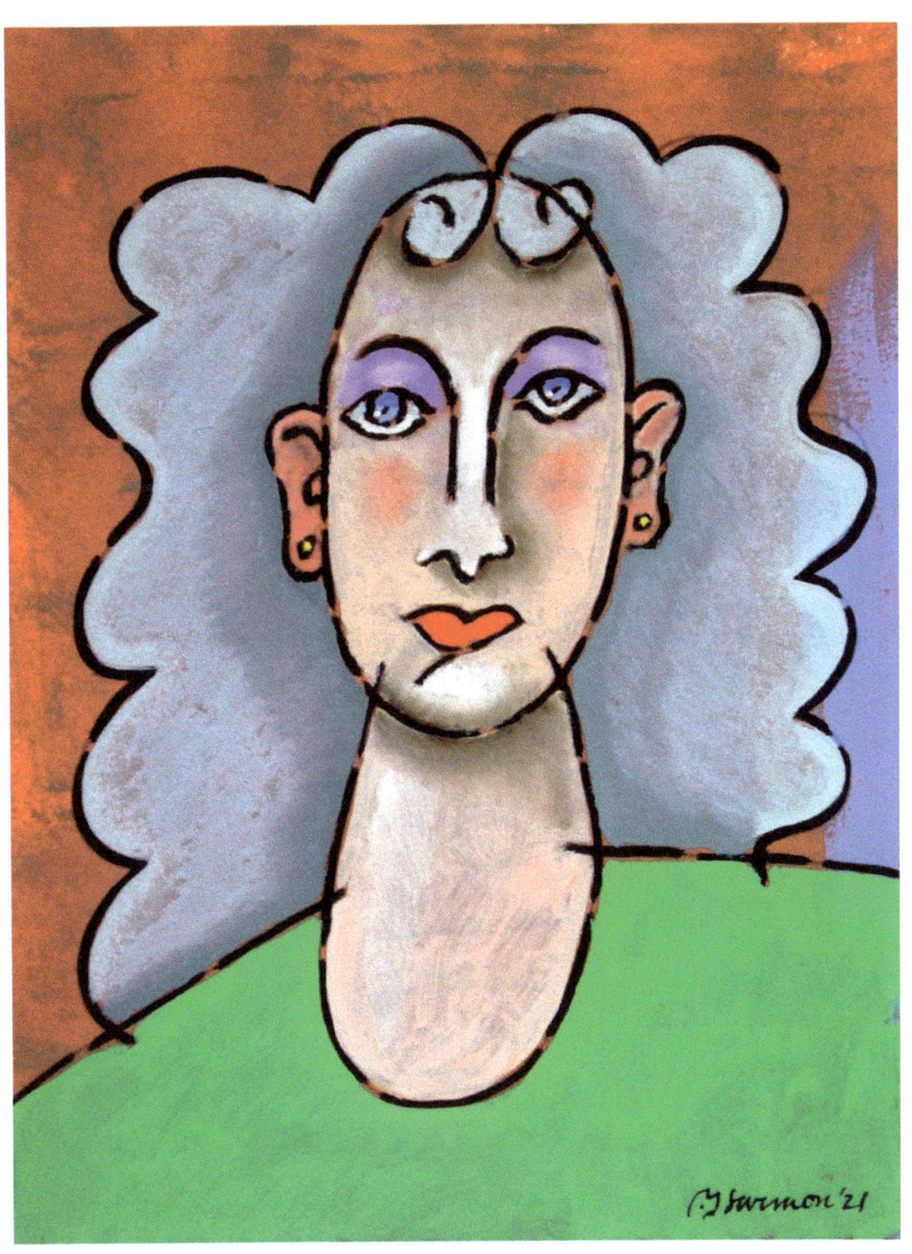
B Harmon '21

In general,
My paintings are a personal journey of my life.
The work is therefore both serious
And frivolous, joyous,
And melancholic, spiritual, and erotic.
The continuity is in the fact
That it tracks a real life.

Paul Harmon

Double Down. Beliefs Wear Crowns
At The Door Of Reality's Store.
Forget The Blame. Jesus Did The Same.
Thoughts Like Rain Can Turn Into Religious Trains.
Controlled Gain In Flowering Pain.
Degeneration Switch Does The Flip When
Weary Bones Groan And Take Back Their Throne.
Moments Of Stress Are No Longer Guests.
Backdoor Light. Fear Runs From Sight.
Cause Psycho-Time Is A Mighty Find.
Riches Dress In A Happy Mess.
Cells Don't Mind.
Regeneration Broom Cleans The Room.
It Shakes The Air
With Electromagnetic Flair
Singed
In Grey Hair.

HTM

If you believe firmly that your consciousness
Is locked up somewhere inside your skull
And is powerless to escape it.
And if you feel that your consciousness
Ends at the boundary of your body,
Then you sell yourself short.

Seth

There are things
I don't understand about my work,
And it is in that chasm
That I feel my love
For the process increase.

Paul Harmon

In your light I learn how to love;
In your beauty, how to make poems.
You dance inside of my chest,
Where no one sees you,
But sometimes I do,
And that sight
Becomes this art.

Rumi

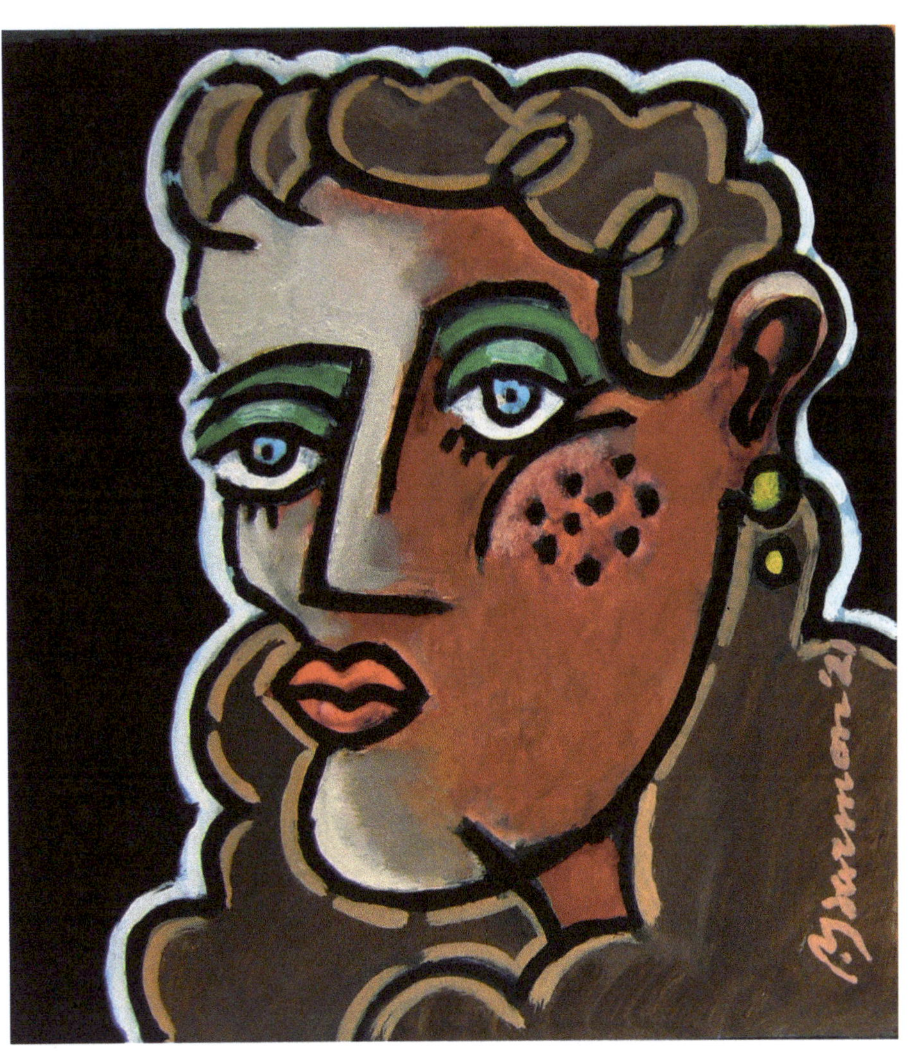

If poetry is an art attempting
To put words to the things
That have no words,
Then what can a painting be?
At any rate, I cannot think of painting
Without thinking first about poetry.

Paul Harmon

The first important step is to realize
That your beliefs about reality are just that—
Beliefs About reality
And not necessarily attributes of reality.
You must make a clear distinction
Between you and your beliefs.
You must then realize
Your beliefs are physically materialized.
What you believe to be true in your experience
IS true.

Seth

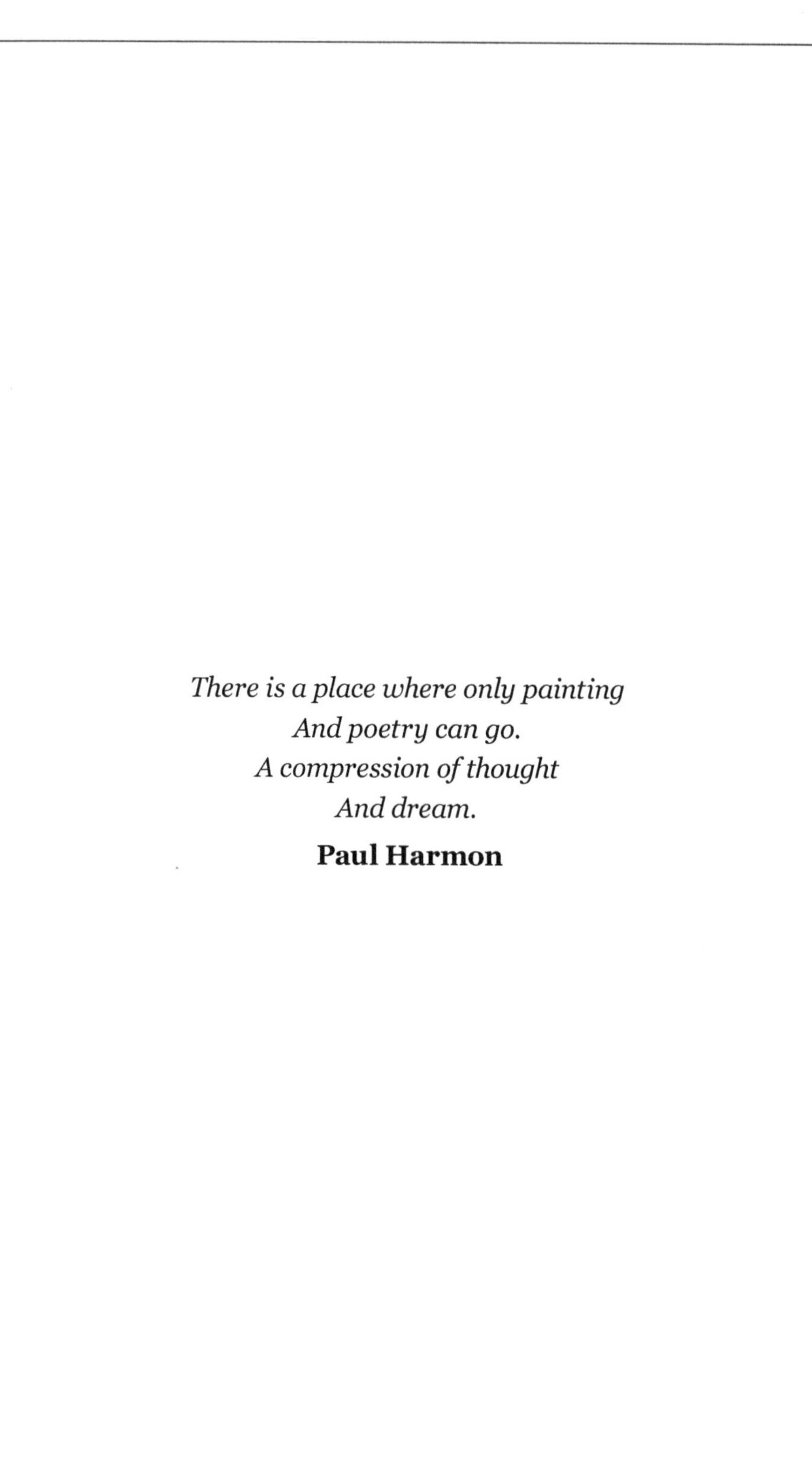

There is a place where only painting
And poetry can go.
A compression of thought
And dream.

Paul Harmon

Owls On The Hill
Morse-Coding Their Thrills.
Dove Fly By And Senses Why.
Rabbit's On A Stump
In A Pellet Dump—
Hears A Thump On Its Rump.
Hard To See
When Beliefs Act Like Bees.
Stinging Minds In Perception Time.
Nature's Roast Is An Innate
Fulfillment Toast.

HTM

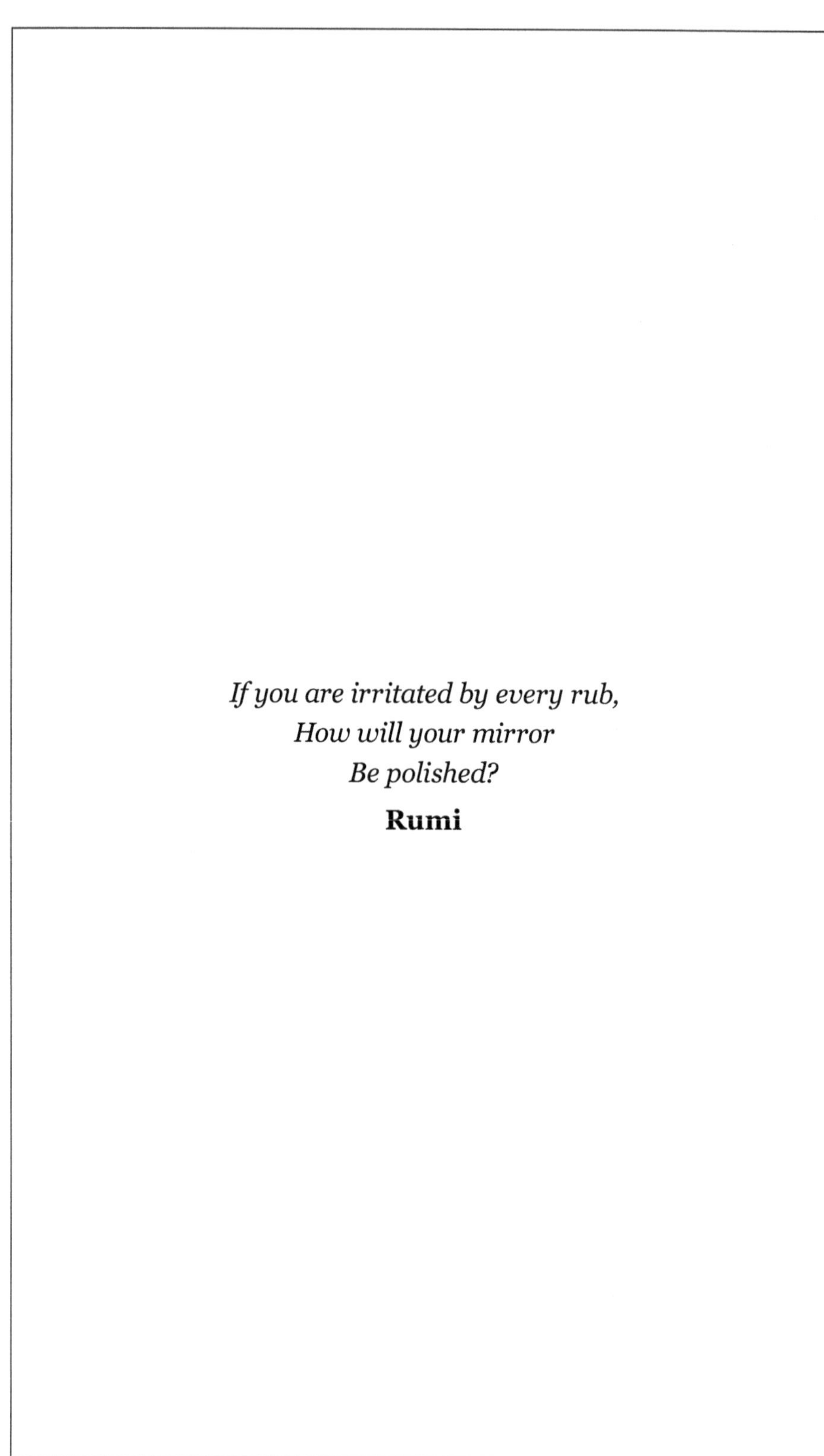

If you are irritated by every rub,
How will your mirror
Be polished?

Rumi

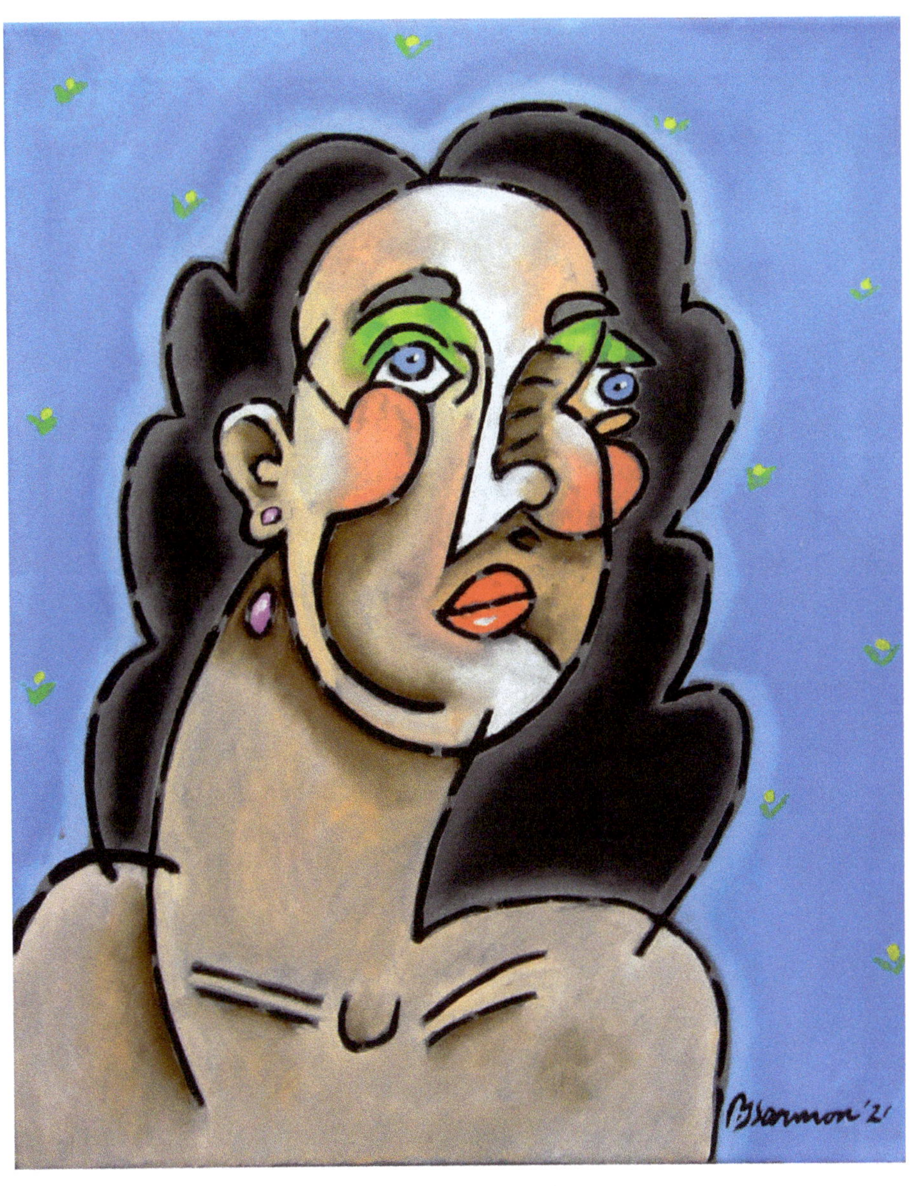
BHarmon '21

Themes in my painting keep reoccurring
But in slightly different form.
Like life itself,
This is a circular voyage.

Paul Harmon

Lots Of Slips And Energy Dips.
Never Know The Time
In A Constant Rewind.
Thoughts Like To Splice
The Good And Nice
For A Seat In The Drama Beat.
Not Too Tall. Choices Can Crawl
Under A Seat
Where Beliefs Meet.

HTM

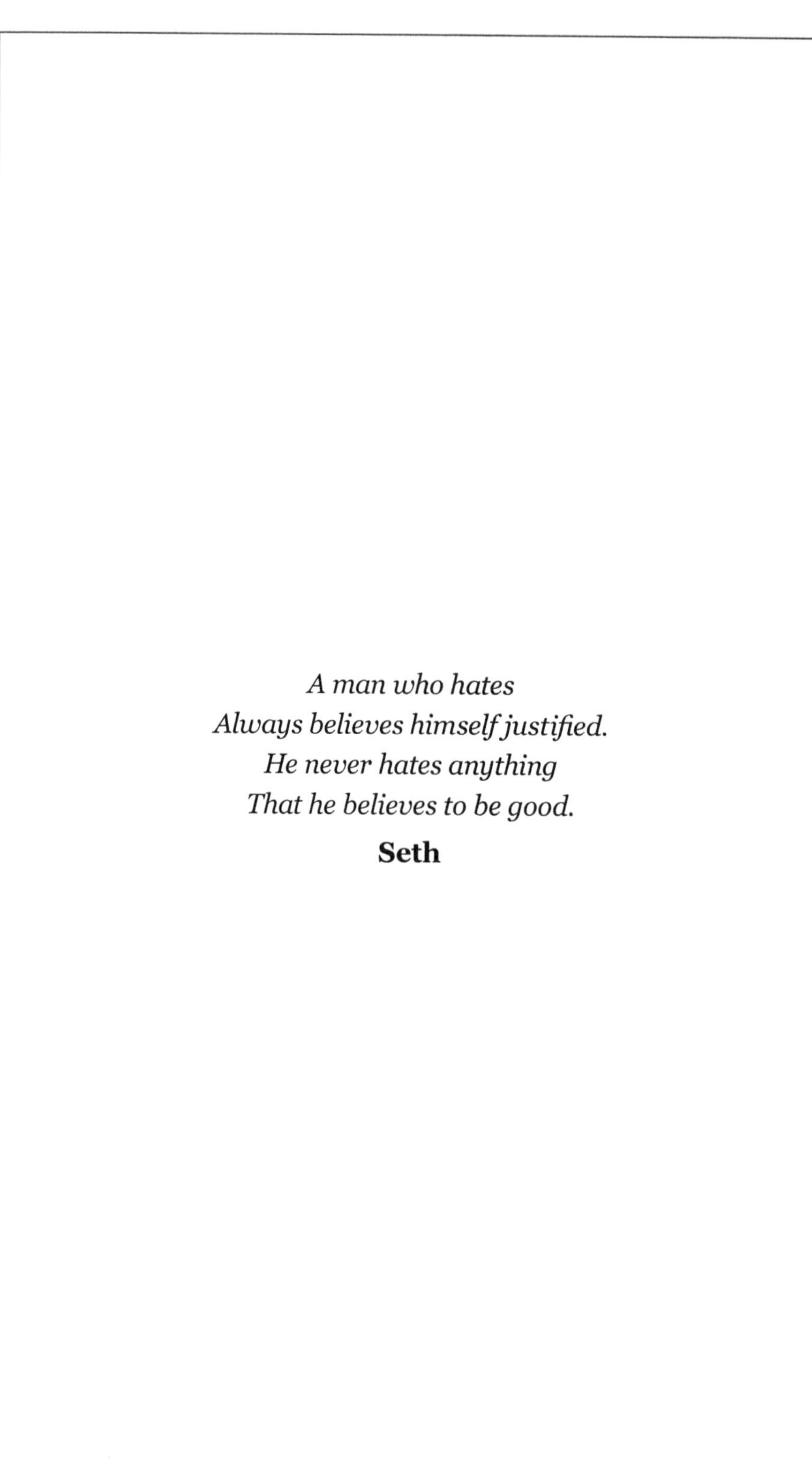

A man who hates
Always believes himself justified.
He never hates anything
That he believes to be good.

Seth

Be it in a painting —
As in relationships—
We wish pleasure,
But also meaning.

Paul Harmon

Do you think I know what I am doing?
That for one breath or half-breath
I belong to myself?
As much as a pen knows what it is writing
Or a ball
Can guess where it is going next.

Rumi

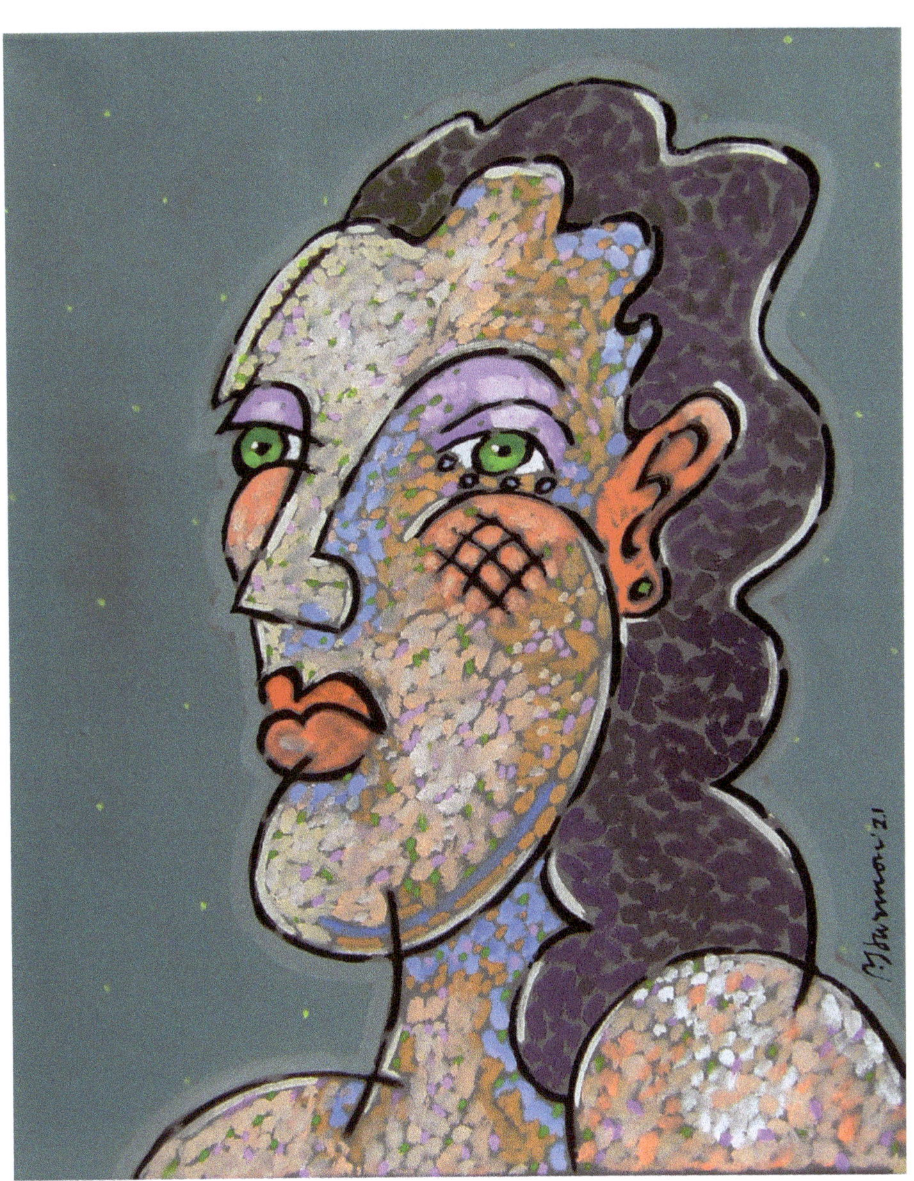

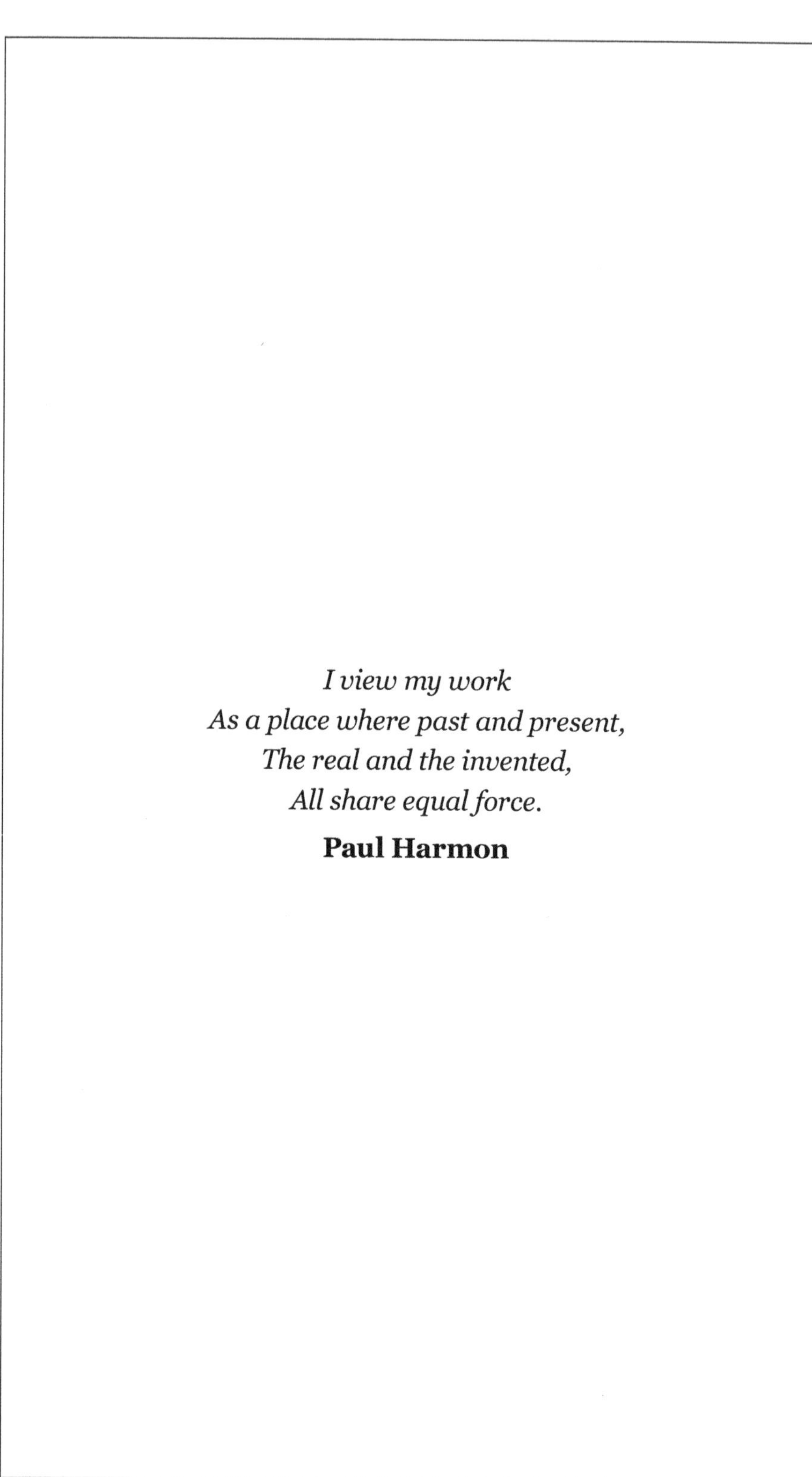

I view my work
As a place where past and present,
The real and the invented,
All share equal force.

Paul Harmon

Jungle Of The Giants Survival In Compliance.
You Tricked Yourself Being Stealth
On A Political Shelf.
Bank Roll's Fat. So Is The Cat.
Social Graces Have Many Faces.
You Want More?
Greed Has A Swinging Door.
Cells Know Well There's No Peace
In Holy Hell
With One-Way Gears.
And A Fear-Laced Spear.

HTM

Two Cats On A Mat
Scratching Each Other's Back.
Paws With Claws Get Applause
When Truth Hits A Wall
Anchored To A Tree
Home Of Killer Bees.
Plenty Of Room.
Rabbits In The Grass.
Leaves Up The Ass.
Forked Branches
Come From
Energy Ranches.
All Of This
In A Psychic Bun.
Blasting Out
Perception Fun.

HTM

Freedom is the inner realization
That you are an individual.
That you do create your reality,
That you do have the freedom. . .
And the joy. . .
And the responsibility
Of forming the physical reality in which you live.
Then you can change the reality.

Seth

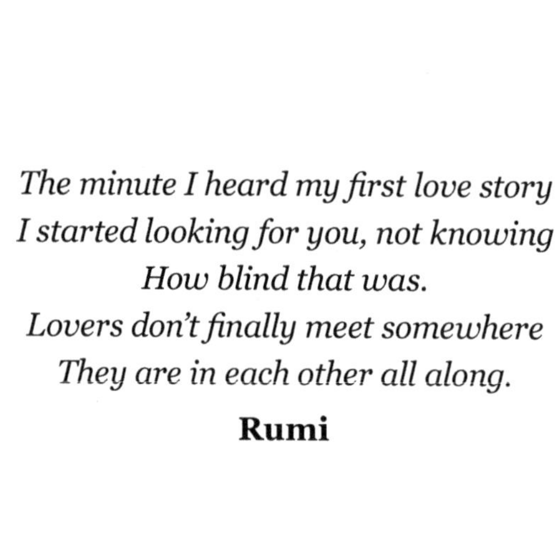

The minute I heard my first love story
I started looking for you, not knowing
How blind that was.
Lovers don't finally meet somewhere
They are in each other all along.

Rumi

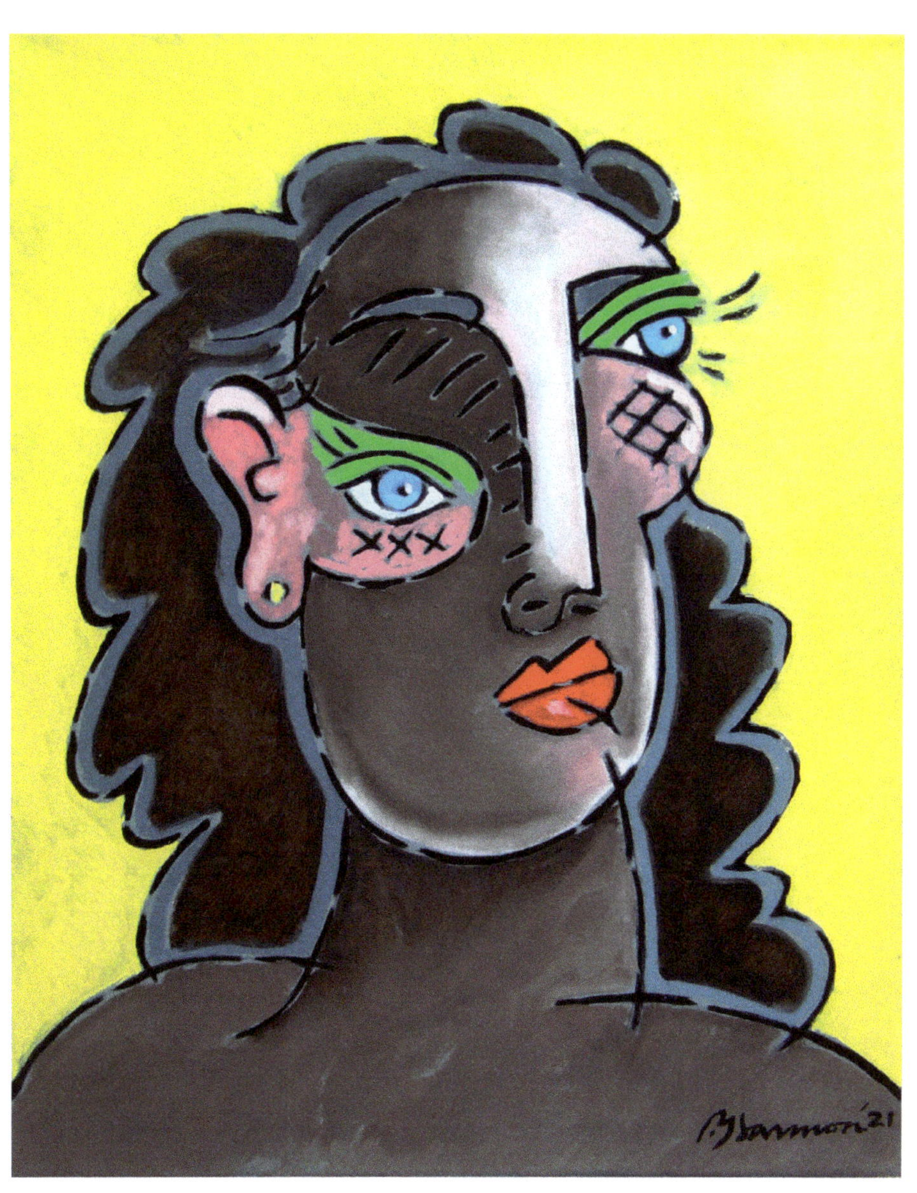
BHarmon '21

The secret (I think) is to absorb
All possible from our heroes,
For however long it takes,
And then at some time
In our life. . .
To leave them and concentrate
On making work
That is true to ourselves.
Work that pings true
With the tuning fork
That is in every artist.

Paul Harmon

Let us make clear:
Your conscious beliefs
Direct the flow
Of unconscious processes
Which bring your ideas
Into physical reality,
So while your thoughts cause
Your experience,
You are NOT
Consciously aware
Of how
This takes place.

Seth

When you love others,
You grant them their innate freedom
And do not cravenly insist
That they always attend you.
There are no divisions to love.
There is no basic difference
Between the love
Of a child for a parent,
A parent for a child,
A wife for a husband,
A brother for a sister.
There are only various expressions
And characteristics of love.
And, all love affirms.

Seth

A painting is not a thing to figure out.
It is not a riddle or a puzzle.
Like music, it is something to experience.
Allow it to wash over you.

Paul Harmon

There is life-force within your soul,
Seek that life.
There is a gem in the mountain of your body,
Seek that mine.
O traveler if you are in search of That
Don't look outside,
Look inside yourself
And seek That.

Rumi

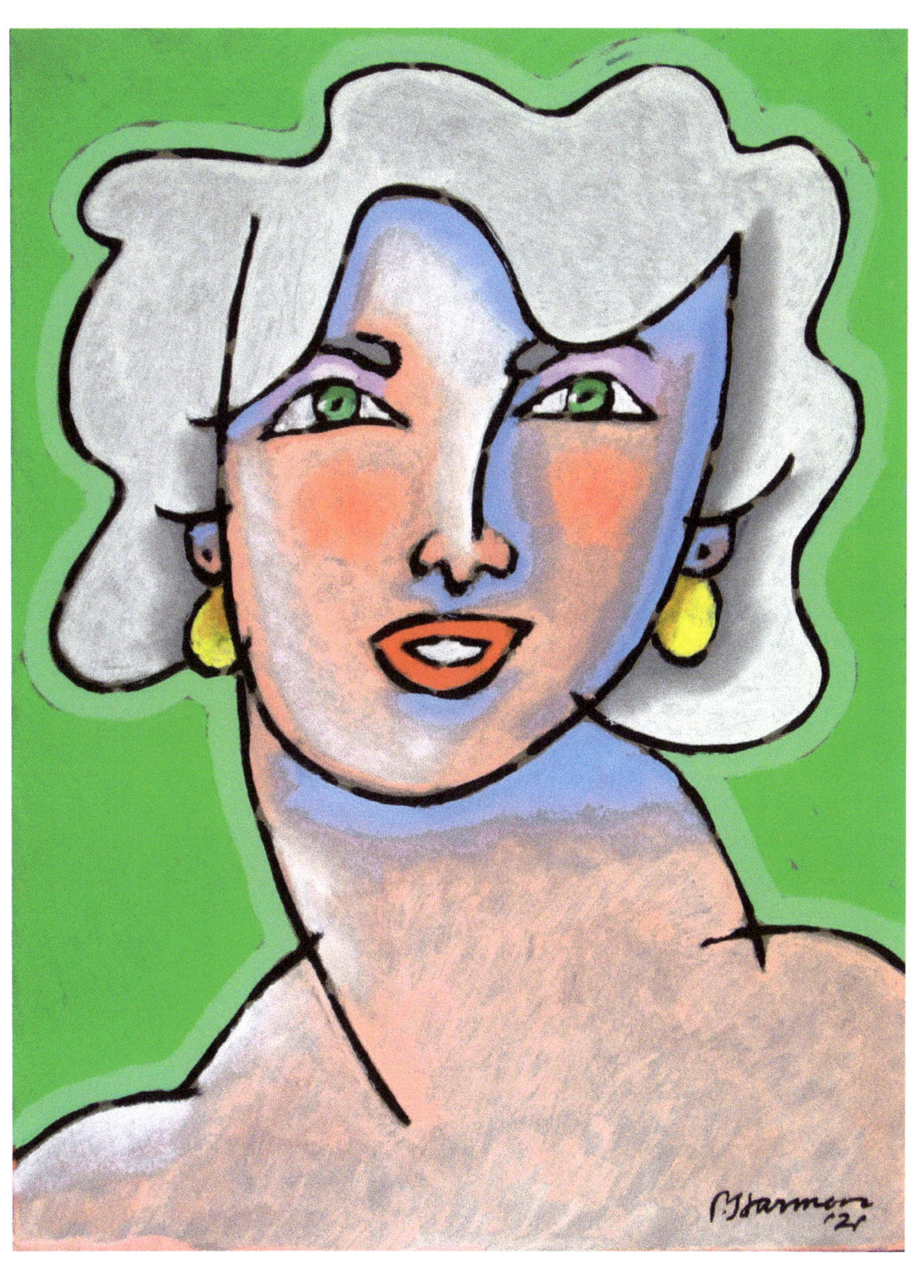

To change your experience
Or any portion of it, you must
change your ideas.
Since you have been forming
Your own reality all along,
The results
Will follow naturally.

Seth

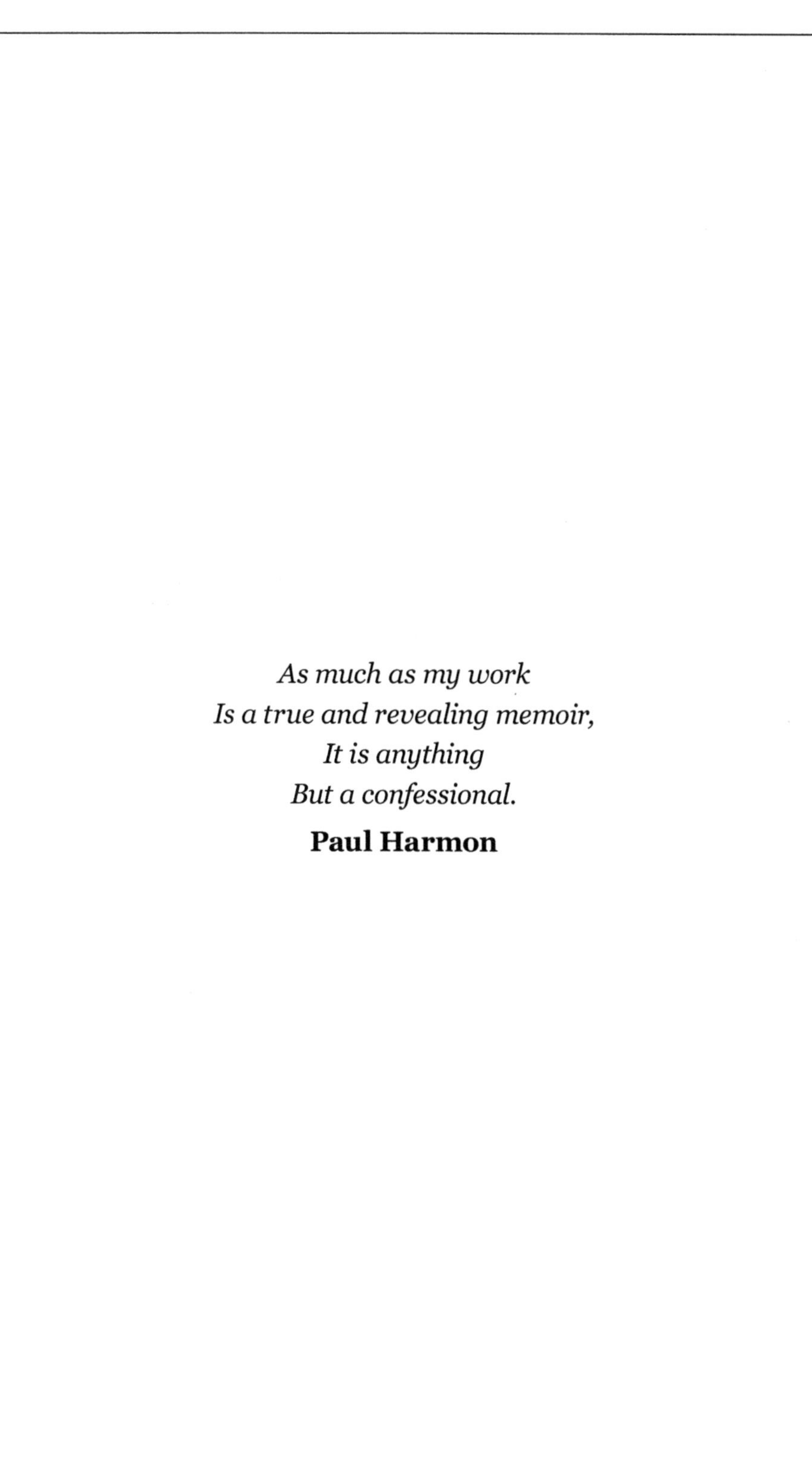

As much as my work
Is a true and revealing memoir,
It is anything
But a confessional.

Paul Harmon

Plato was wrong. Art is not a lie. . .
The copy of a copy.
The idea of the gods having made the original,
Nature making the first copy,
And man making a copy of nature.

Art is a thing unto itself.
It honors creation and nature and the gods
By being a true thing on its own.

Paul Harmon

Open That Door. Body Language Keeps Score.
Aches And Pains? Muscles Need A Flame.
Proof's In The Pudding
When The Belly Looks For Filling.
Move And Block Thoughts That Burn
And Choices That Confirm
A One Track Mind Lost In Time.
Mental Block. Beliefs Act Like Rocks.
That Pull Perceptions Round The Clock
In An Inner
Nowhere Tick-Tock.

HTM

Look at this cup that can hold the ocean.
Look at those who see the face.
Look through friends' eyes
Into the water that is
Entirely jewels.

Rumi

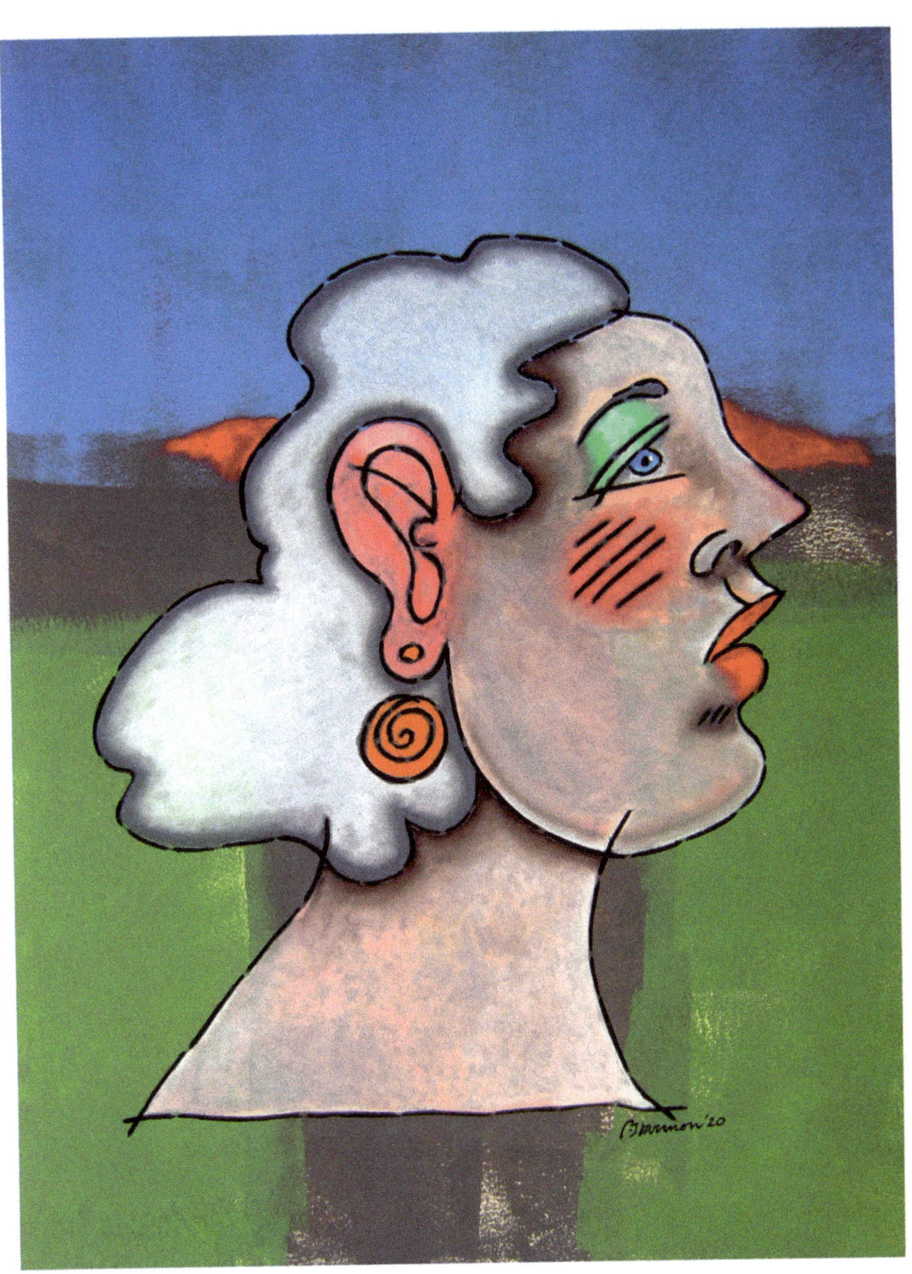

I have found nothing in my work that is not clearly in Dante.
One of my several intentions is that each painting be a poem. . .
And all my paintings from the first to the last,
Be autobiography.

Paul Harmon

You are unknowingly immersed
In and a part of pure energy,
Being newly created in each moment,
So that the energy of your atoms and molecules
And of your physical universal system
Is being replenished
At every conceivable moment.

Seth

The entryway into physical matter is the ATOM,
And it still resides outside physical reality
In the spacious present,
While being within it at the same time—
Which is true of everything,
Of course, including us.

Seth

Owls On The Prowl
Tom Cat Says Meow.
Land On The Take
Perception Has No Brakes.
Anger Rules When
Rumors And Labels
Turn The Tables.
Nothing Seems Right
When Fear Takes A Bite.
Rattled Bones. Beliefs Are Drones
That Capture Choices
With Similar Voices.

HTM

When you are with everyone but me,
You're with no one.
When you are with no one but me,
You're with everyone.
Instead of being so bound up with everyone,
Be everyone.
When you become that many,
You're nothing.
Empty.

Rumi

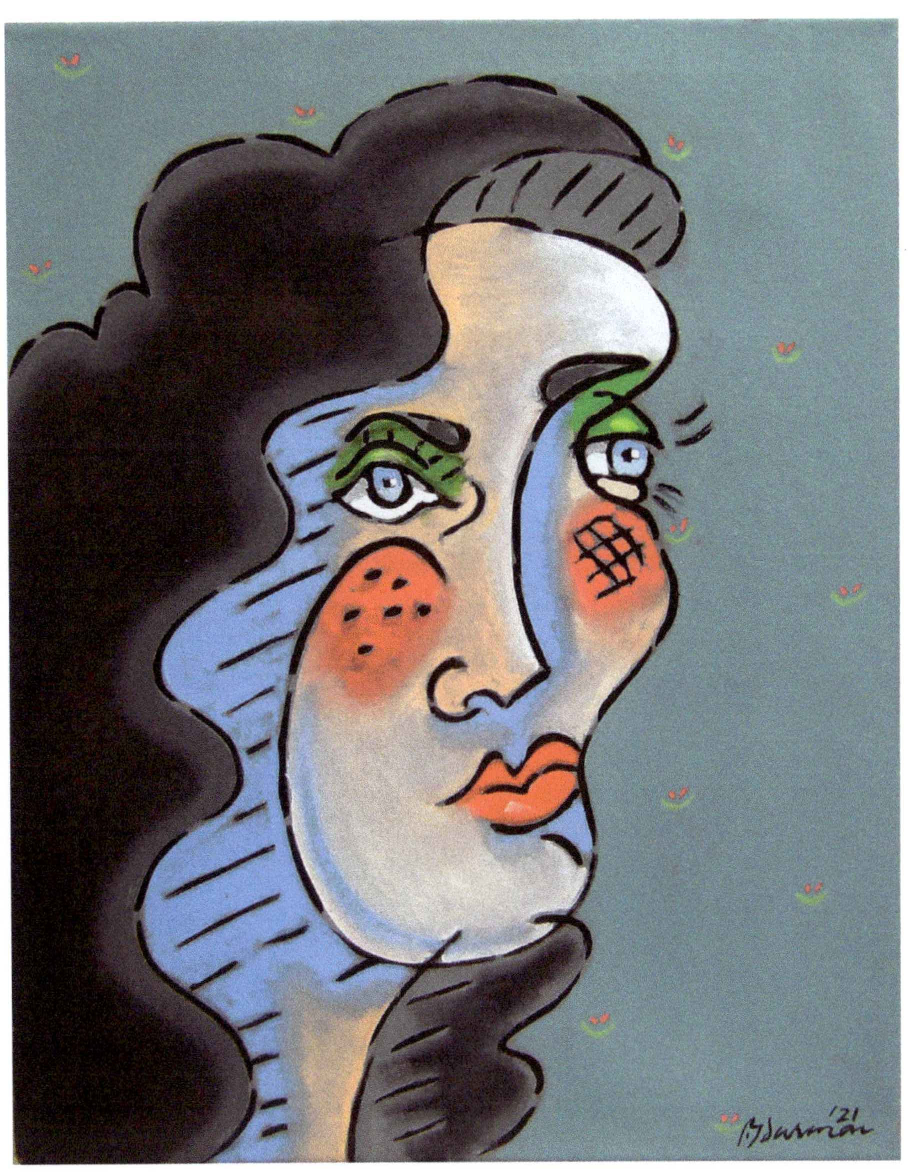

Instructive, the early work of an artist,
In that it shows the sprouts from which
May grow
A full-blown body of serious
And personal creation.
Looking at much of the work from the 60s and 70s,
I see myself in search of a stencil.

Paul Harmon

Because your imagination follows your beliefs
You can find yourself in a vicious circle
In which you constantly paint pictures
In your mind that Reinforce "negative" aspects in your life.
The imaginative events generate appropriate emotions,
Which automatically bring about hormonal changes
In your body
Or affect your behavior with others,
Or cause you to interpret events
Always in the light of your beliefs.

Seth

Plenty Of Years Lots Of Cheers.
Loads Of Love In A Psyche Memory Tub.
Time Has A Perception Glow
When Choices Hit The Lights
Like Captain Midnight.
Anger Float By
In A Meandering Sky.
Rich In Fables Dressed In Labels.
Beliefs Build A Cable
To Reality's Fable.

HTM

We are all vapor, smoke, transparent cosmos.
Something not even atmosphere.
It is untouchable and unseeable.
Only our sense of self
Can know of its existence.
But it is real.

Paul Harmon

Little by little wean yourself.
This is the gist of what I have to say.
From an embryo,
Whose nourishment comes in the blood,
Move to an infant drinking milk,
To a child on solid food,
To a searcher after wisdom,
To a hunter of more invisible game.

Rumi

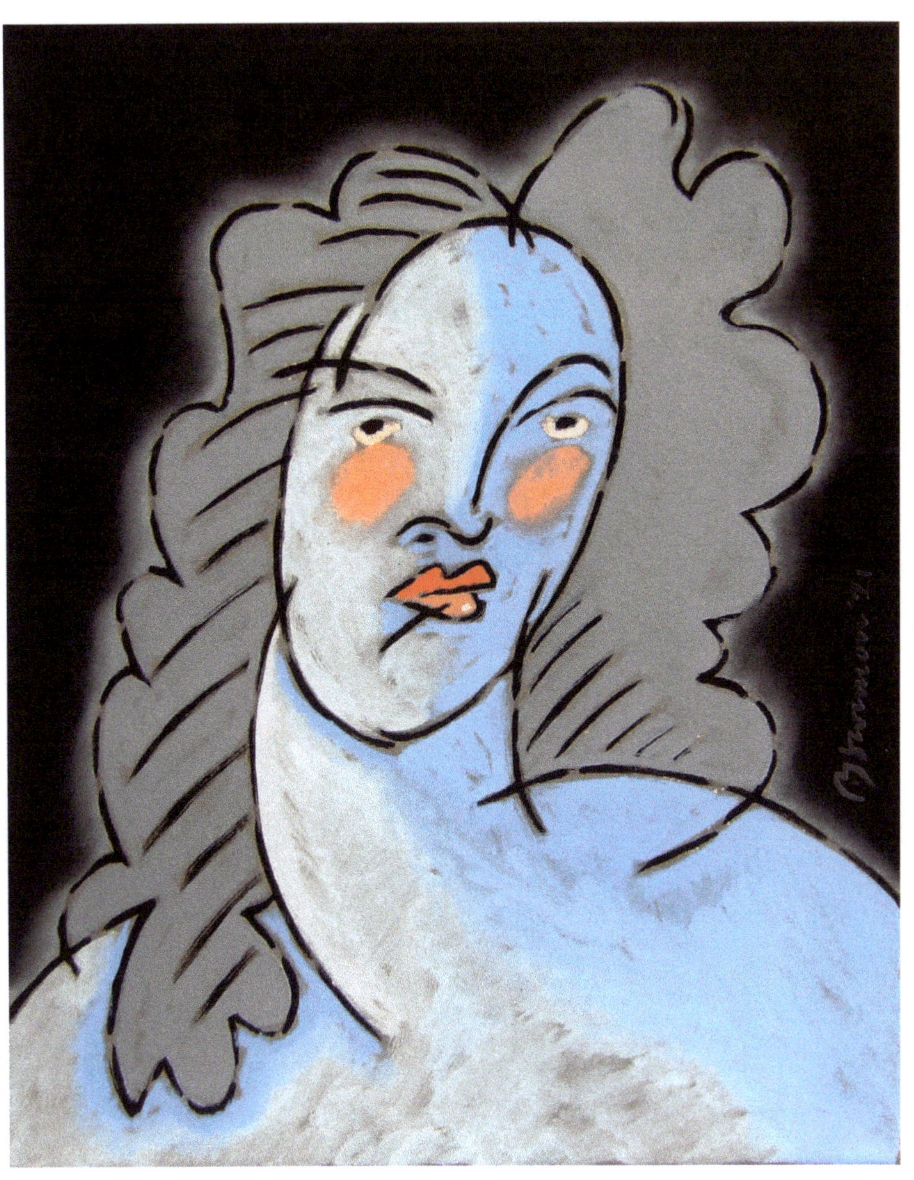

Photographs are spoken of as images
Frozen in time.
In my Paintings,
I think of the images
As either in the process of arriving
Or in a state of disappearing.

Paul Harmon

Ego Surprise. Beliefs Take Brides.
What's It Going To Be?
Chaos And Misery
Or
A Self Getting Dressed
And Unraveling The Mess?
It's A Pity Tune
When You Move Truth
From Room To Gloom.
Where Gospels Speak And People Leap
Into The Charm Of Fear's
Open Arms.

HTM

All of existence and consciousness is interwoven.
Only when you think of the soul
As something different,
Separate,
And therefore closed
Are you led to consider a separate god—
A personality that seems
To be apart from creation.

Seth

A painting should have a vitality
That is no mere reflection
Of external reality.
A painting must
Inherently have a reality of its own.
Its genetics must
Be unique from the artist.

Paul Harmon

Super Cells Thoughts Do Tell
Beliefs Control Your Body Mode.
Cracks In The Road Memories Explode
Like A Petri Dish Full
Of Judgmental Fish.
Take Off The Hat
Nerves Need Some Slack.
Pull Off Those
One-Sided Perception Boards.
Where Beliefs Like To Hoard
Roots That Leak
From Thoughts
That Squeak.

HTM

I like a stencil-like line.
The openness allows my subjects to be symbols
For a thing vs. the specific thing.
And the difference between literature and song
And my work
Is simply the medium
And the tools.

Paul Harmon

In love
There is no high or low,
No bad behavior, no good behavior.
No leader, no follower, no devotee;
Just indifference,
Tolerance
And giving up.

Rumi

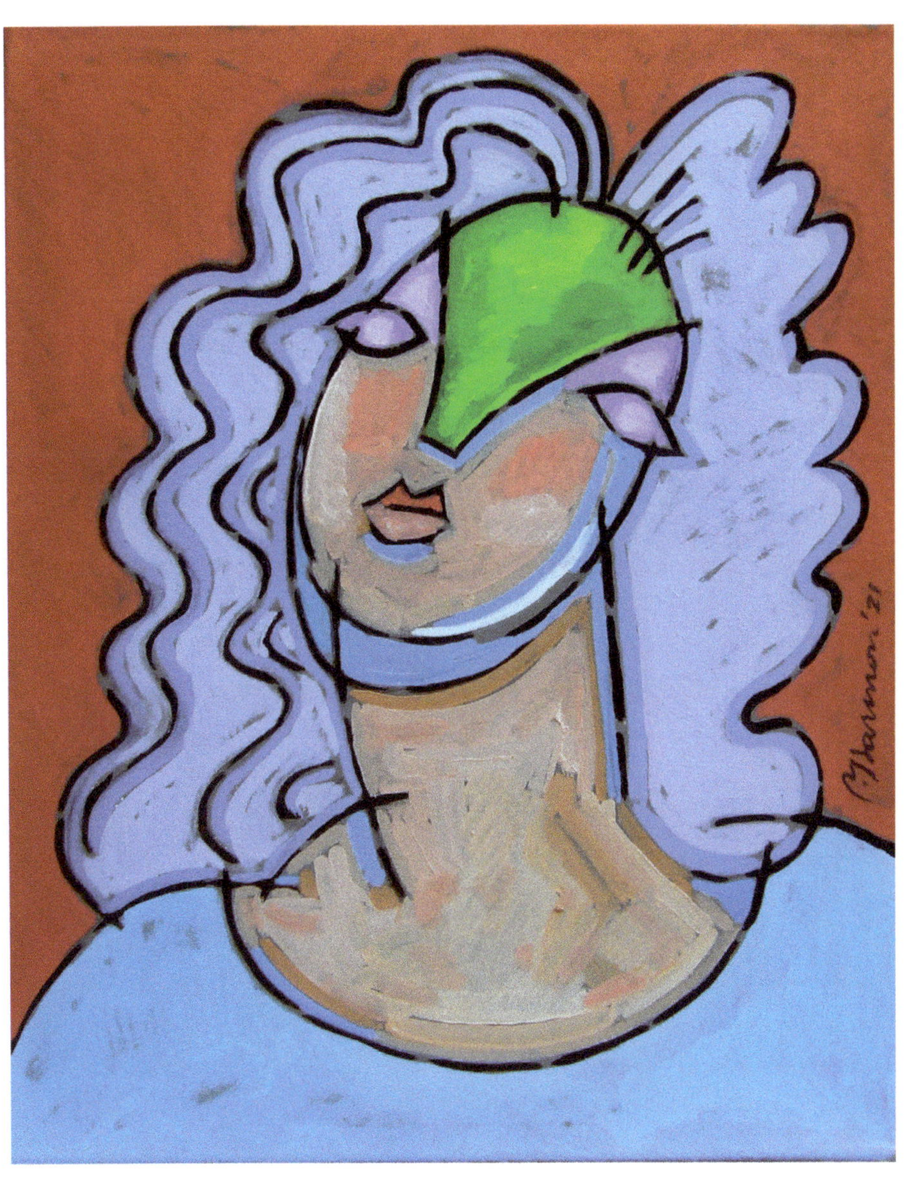

Examine all of your beliefs about yourself
And the nature of reality;
And one belief, if you let it,
Will lead you to another.
Imagination and will power
Are never in conflict.
Your beliefs may conflict,
But your imagination
Will always follow your will power
And your conscious thoughts
And beliefs.

Seth

My Best studio hours are those
Between midnight and dawn.
It's easier to gather
All those long dead artists and writers
In those hours.
There is nothing remotely lonely
About painting
All night in my studio.

Paul Harmon

Many people believe fervently
That with approaching age
They will meet a steady, disastrous
Deterioration in which the senses
And the mind will be dull,
And the body, stricken with disease,
Will lose all of its vigor and aging.

Many young people believe such nonsense
And therefore they set themselves up
To meet the very conditions, they fear.
The mind grows wiser with age
When it is allowed to do so.

Seth

With all my talking
About my work,
It doesn't betray
What I profoundly know.
That core
Which cannot be expressed.

Paul Harmon

Poems reach up
Like spindrift and the edge
Of driftwood along the beach,
Wanting!
They derive from a slow
And powerful root
That we can't see.
Stop the words now.
Open the window in the center
Of your chest,
And let the spirits
Fly in and out.

Rumi

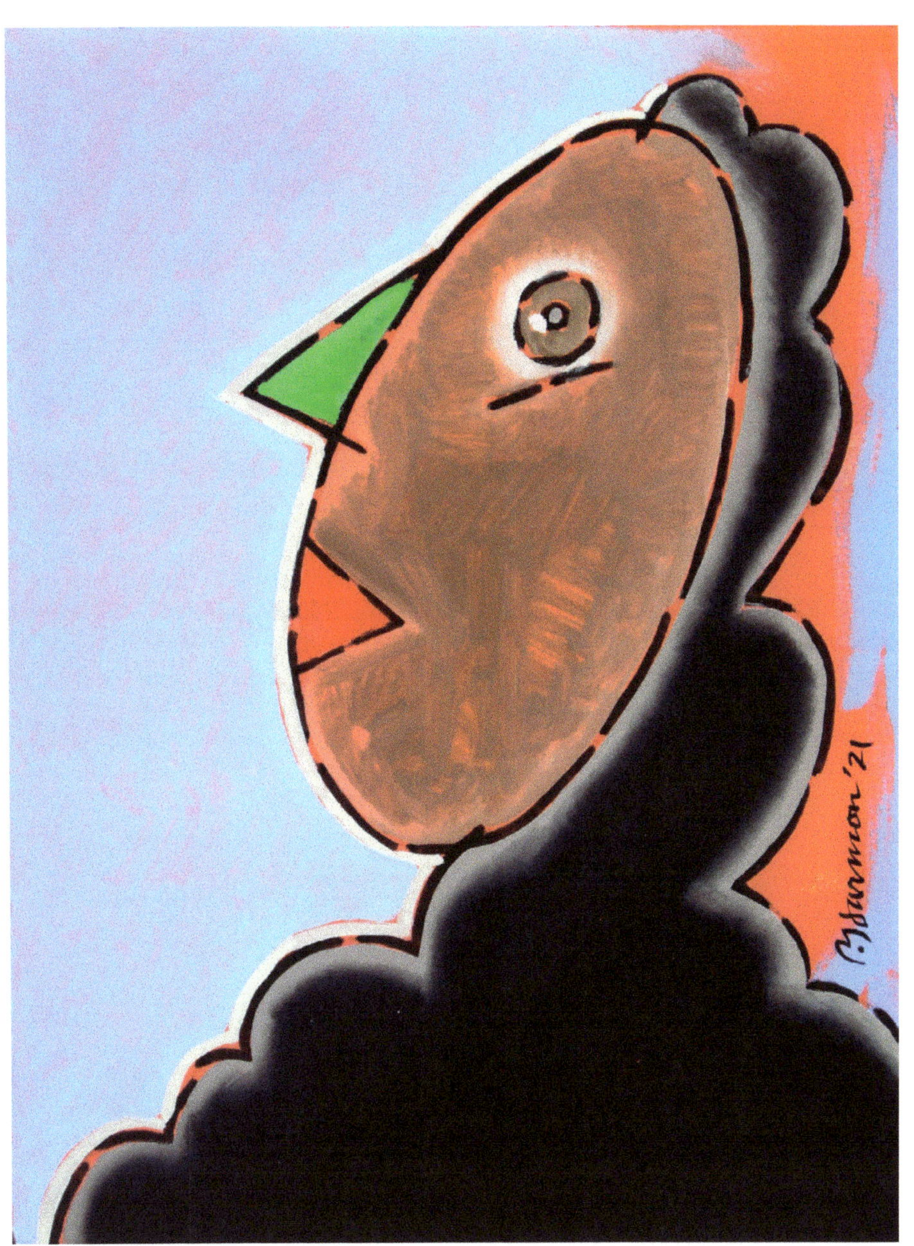

Physically speaking,
Man's 'purpose' is to help enrich the quality
Of existence
In all of its dimensions.

Spiritually speaking,
His 'purpose' is to understand
The qualities of love and creativity,
To intellectually and psychically understand
The sources of his being,
And to lovingly create
Other dimensions of reality
Of which
He is presently unaware.

Seth

Victim Of Time In The Mortal Mind.
Puffs of Clouds Swirling Round
Open Your Mental Gate
Energy Likes To Mate.
Age Is A Test Not A Regress
When You Know You Create This
Physical Dream Show.
Thoughts Are Symbols. Perceptions Nimble.
When Old Beliefs Start To Crease
And The Self Delivers A Pass
To Freedom At Last.

HTM

You expect the cells of your body
To be replaced.
You expect your image
To continue day by day,
Although the physical matter
Of your image today
Has not one atom
Or molecule within it
That was a portion of your image
Ten years ago.

The bodies that you had
Ten years ago
Are dead and gone,
And you never missed them,
And you do not feel dead.

Seth

Stranglehold Tight. Natural Might.
Smell The Wind. Feel It Spin.
Embrace The Cold You're Never Old
Said A Man In Glacier Land.
Grab A Cloud. Laugh Out Loud.
Be A Tree. Leaf With Glee.
Lift A Stone That's Heaven Prone.
Dance On Grass?
Bet Your Ass!
Kiss Your Clone. Life's A Special Throne.
Climb The Hill Forget The Pills.
Mind's Got A Shovel
For All Kinds Of Trouble.
Stashed Away
In A Non-Physical Way.

HTM

There is a community of spirit.
Join in, and feel the delight
Of walking in the noisy street,
And being the noise.

Rumi

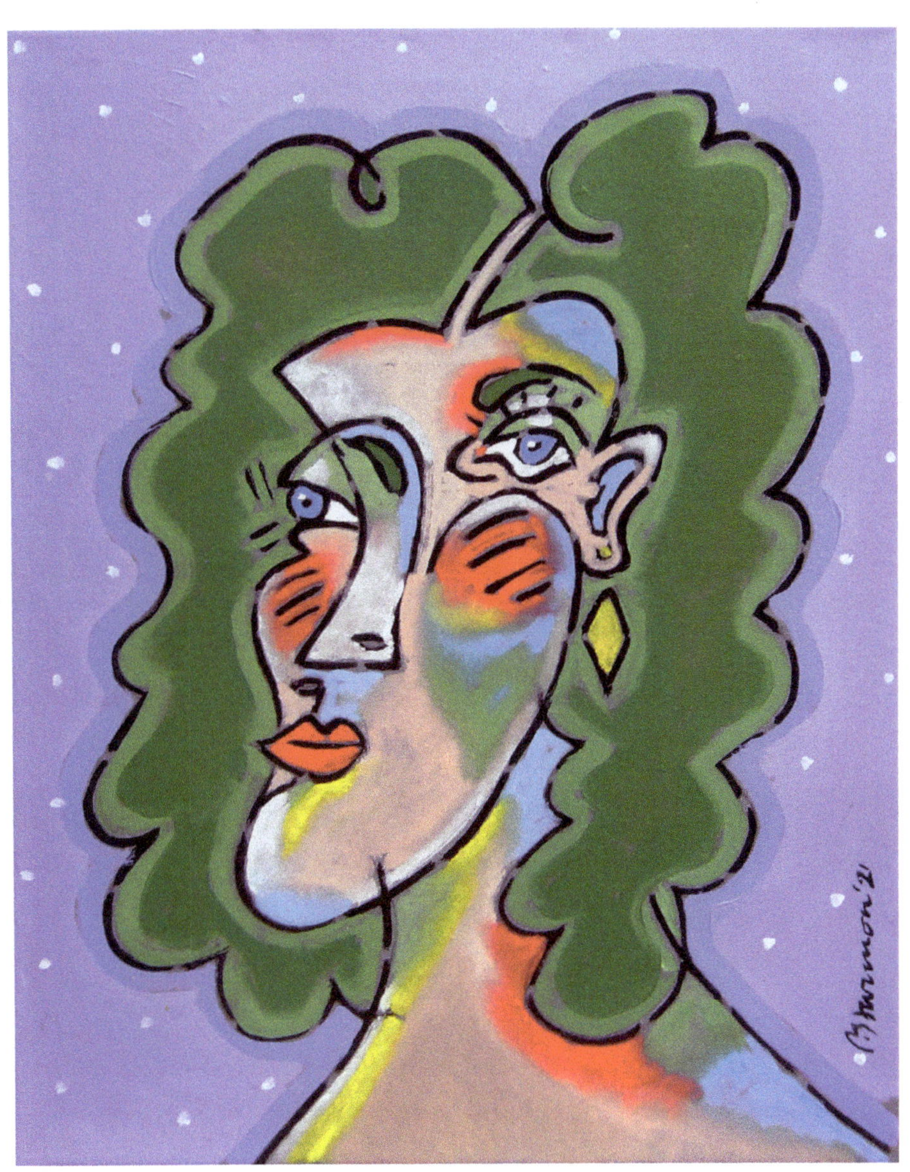

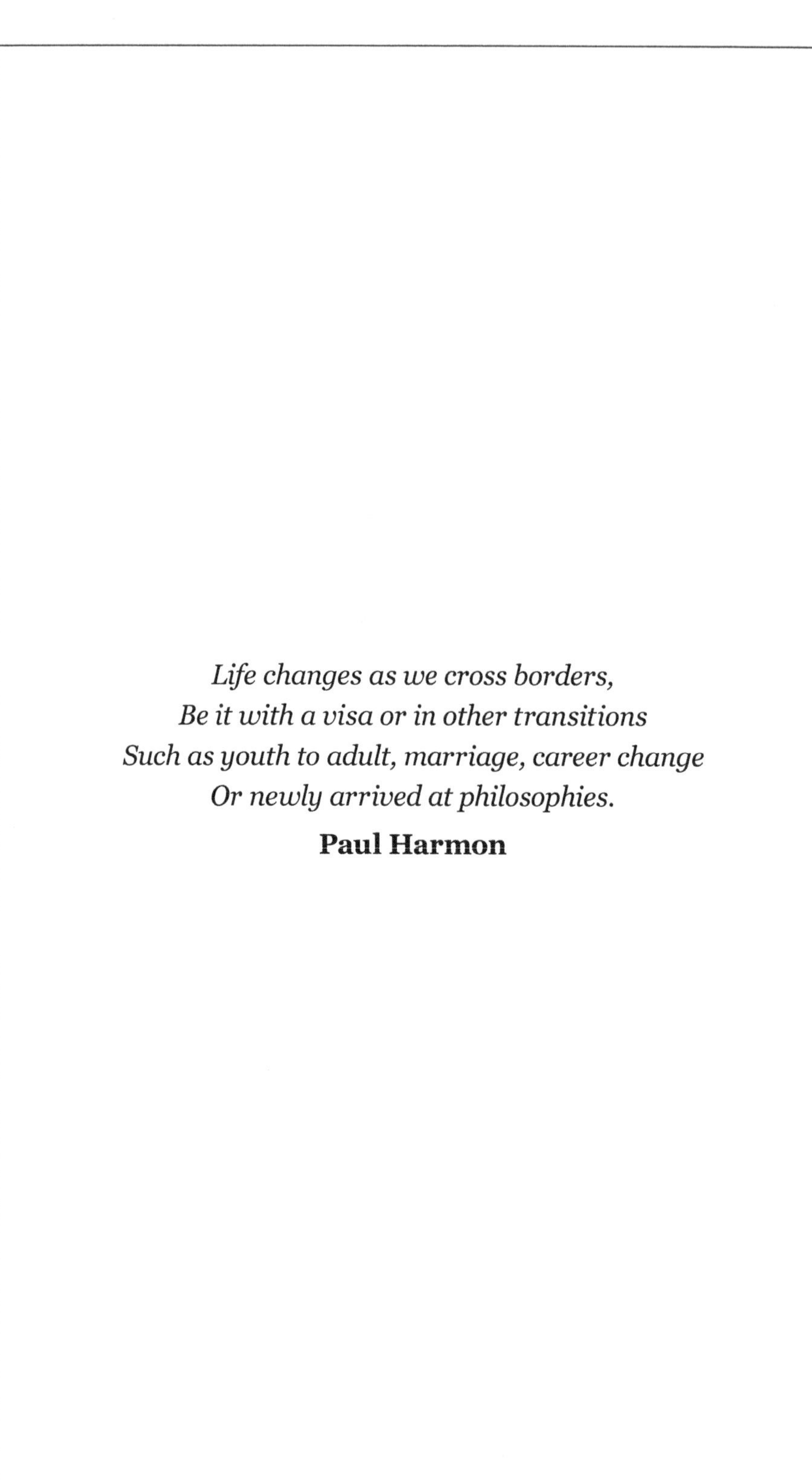

Life changes as we cross borders,
Be it with a visa or in other transitions
Such as youth to adult, marriage, career change
Or newly arrived at philosophies.

Paul Harmon

At each moment,
From the most microscopic Levels the body
Is ascertaining a constant picture of its position
Within physical reality. (In one way or another)

That picture is composed of millions
Of ever-changing smaller snapshots, as it were—
Or moving pictures is better—
Determining so many conditions,
Positions, and relationships
That they could never be described.

Seth

Memories Are Like The Wind.
They Twist And Swirl Like Psychic Pearls.
Broken Branches Lots Of Chances
Guilt Floats By
With The Usual High.
Imagine A World Where Beliefs
Set The Stage For Constant Gain.
You're In It Man.
Bagged And Tagged
No Reasons Why.
Choices Lie.
But Here It Is—
Thoughts Like Quizzes
And Redo Blisses.

HTM

A painting should be an open window.
Universal.
A painting should include the unknowable,
The ephemeral,
The ethereal,
The transient
And the accidental.
A painting should mimic
The human DNA.
Paintings
Should be about plurality.

Paul Harmon

A thought comes
Like an honored guest
Into your heart.
My soul, regard each thought
As a person,
For every person's value
Is in the thought they hold.

Rumi

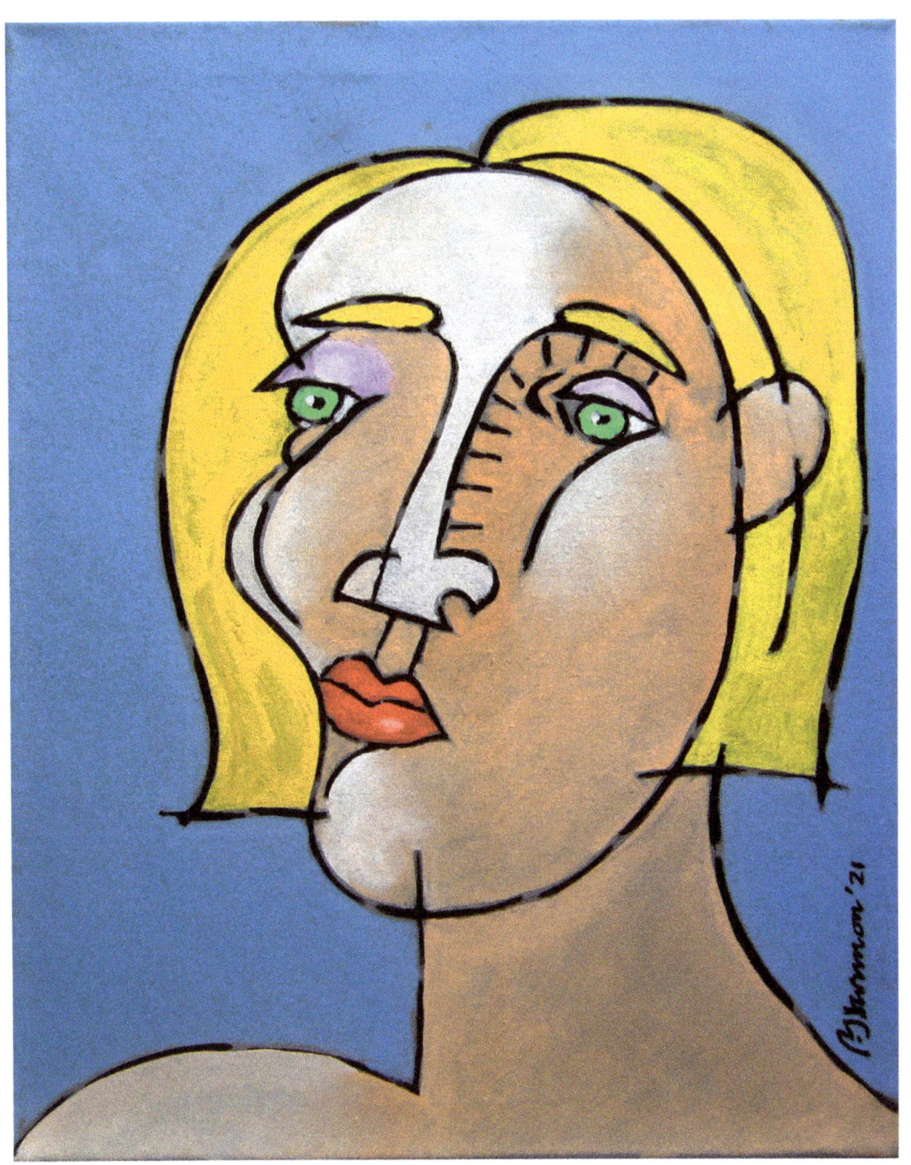

World Of Drama. Belief Pajamas.
Slip On The Ring. Choices Are King
In Reality's Fumbles And Angry Tumbles.
Tail Of The Cold Pansies Stand Bold.
Cracks In The Road Crumble And Erode.
Frozen Beaches In The Land Of Peaches.
Whom To Blame When Thoughts Turn Into Rain.
Where's The Beef In A Changing World Of Grief.
Invest In Cells They Know Full Well
That Annoying Bells Sound Like Hell
When Emotions Crest And Moods Regress
In An Inners Working Test.
Feel The Peel
That's Worth The Deal.
When Life Is
The Essence Of A Squeal.

HTM

Crushed Leaf Flight. Wind's A Kite.
Trees Are Bare In Ruffled Hair.
Grass Lets Out An Ascension Shout!
Thoughts Are Darts. They Hit Their Mark.
In The Till Where Beliefs Chill.
Perceptions Explode. Choices Implode.
In The Arch Of A One-Track Mind
In Holy Time.

HTM

My purpose is not to solve your problems
For you,
But to put you in touch with your own power.
My purpose is not to come
Between you and your own freedom
By giving you 'answers,'
Even to the most tragic of problems.
My purpose is to reinforce your own strength,
For ultimately the magic of your being
Is well equipped to help you find fulfillment,
Understanding, exuberance, and peace.

Seth

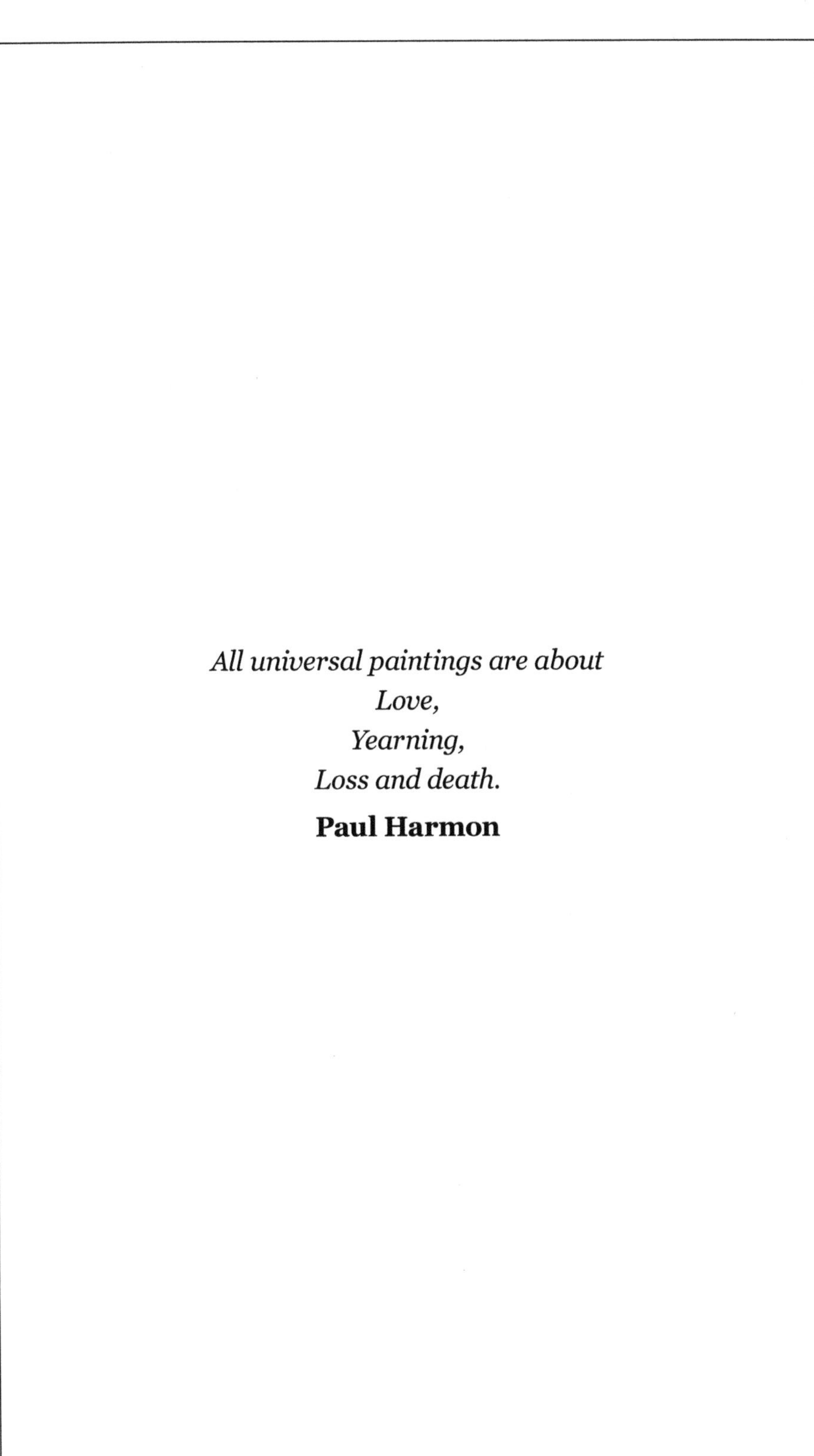

All universal paintings are about
Love,
Yearning,
Loss and death.

Paul Harmon

The breeze at dawn has secrets to tell you
Don't go back to sleep.
You must ask for what you really want.
Don't go back to sleep.
People are going back and forth across the doorsill
Where the two worlds touch.
The door is round and open.
Don't go back to sleep.

Rumi

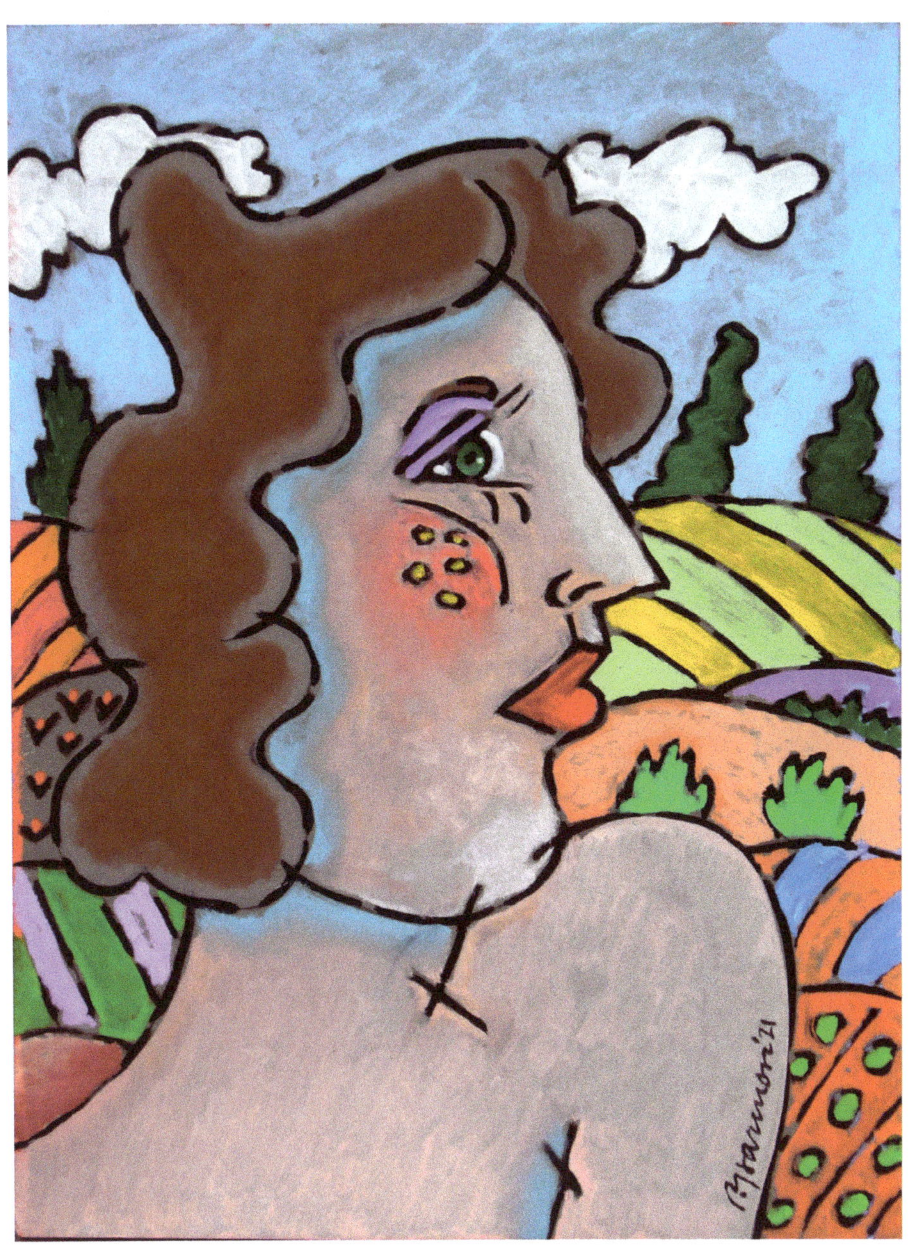

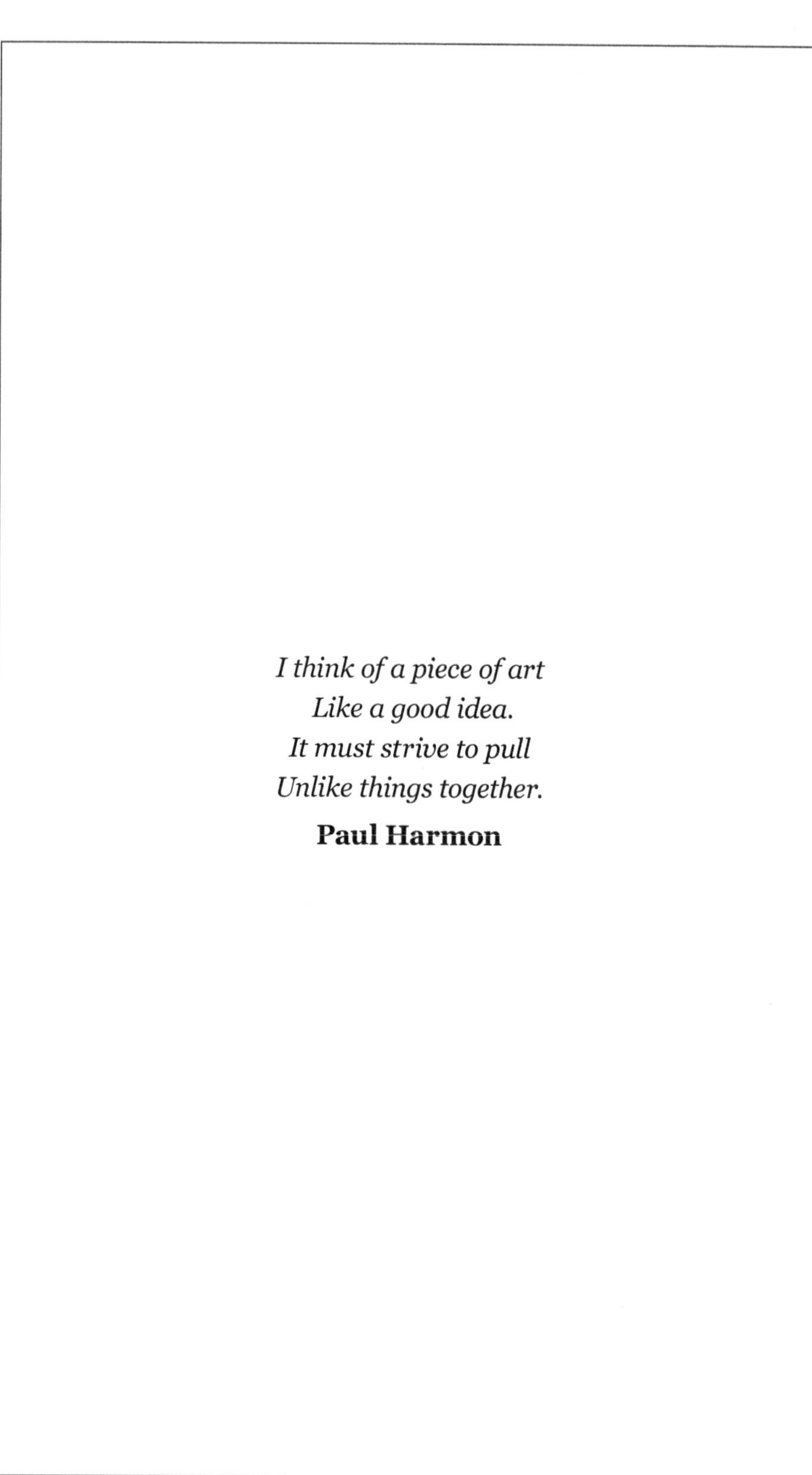

I think of a piece of art
Like a good idea.
It must strive to pull
Unlike things together.

Paul Harmon

You create beliefs
As you go along, in your terms.
Behind all of your beliefs is a reality
Of your being in this moment.
And this moment is eternal and unending.
When I say that,
I do not mean that it is completed
As it is forever.
I mean that it is endlessly creative
And never finished –
Eternally never finished,
But forever growing
As you yourselves are.

Seth

Forward Blows In A Sea Of Woes.
Every Act Is An Anger Attack
On The Cells That Battle Hell.
There's Power In A Crying Hour.
Hit The Floor. Weep A Little More.
Drop The Vest That Says You're A Mess.
Close Those Seams. Juice The Gleam.
Float Like Smoke After A Toke.
Quite Breeze. Sunrise Squeeze.
Day Tripper. Thought Flipper.
You're A Hurricane Force
In Earth's Energy Toss.
Dock The Clock. Drop The Flock.
Truth Tastes Best
With
A Hit Of Zest.

HTM

What I look for in a painting is ambiguity.
One can live with it forever.
The branches lead to infinity of thought.
Certainty ends the exploration.
Certainty shortens the life of the work.
Solution is the death
Of further attention with that work.
Certainty only illustrates.

Paul Harmon

At Breakfast tea a beloved asked her lover,
"Who do you love more, yourself or me?"

From my head to my foot I have become you.
Nothing remains of me but my name.
You have your wish. Only you exist.
I've disappeared like a drop of vinegar
In an ocean of honey.

Rumi

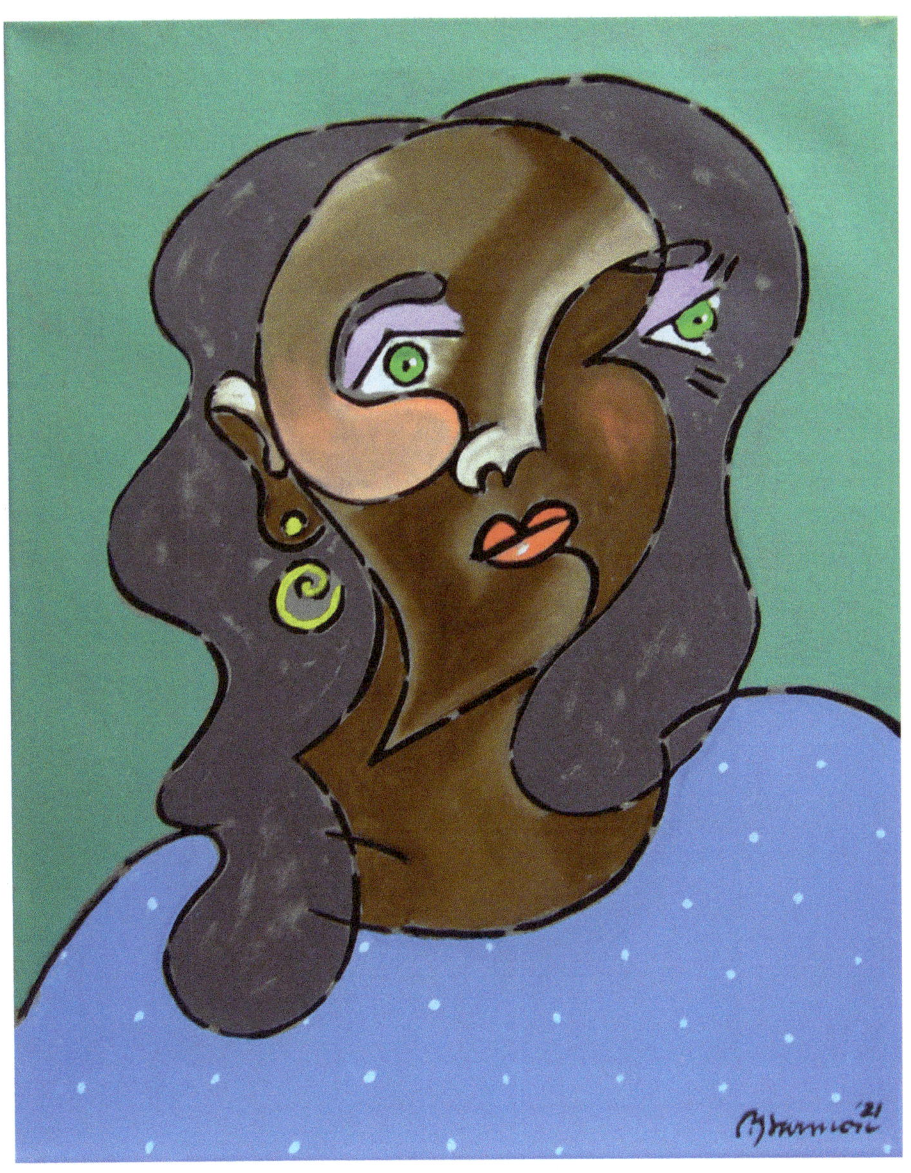

Universality is the goal
Of all my work.
I don't paint things,
But use things as symbols
In reminding us all
Of what it is like
To Be human.
Death is a very important
Aspect of that Largest Equation.

Paul Harmon

Clusters Of Leaves Waltz In The Breeze.
Band's The Rain, With Kick Ass Fame.
Climate Change Is Earth's New Game.
Tornadoes Spin. Drought Steps In.
Temple Bones And Ancient Tones.
Pick Your Spot The World's Hot
And
There's People Art In Ocean Caves.
Forget Quoting Mark.
Time To Build A Mental Arc
With Awareness Love Darts
In A Psychic Letter
Postmarked:
In A Stream
Where
God Screams!

HTM

Love is reckless; not reason.
Reason seeks profit.
Love comes on strong, consuming herself, unabashed.
Yet, in the midst of suffering,
Love proceeds like a millstone,
Hard-surfaced and straightforward.
Having died of self-interest,
She risks everything and asks for nothing.

Rumi

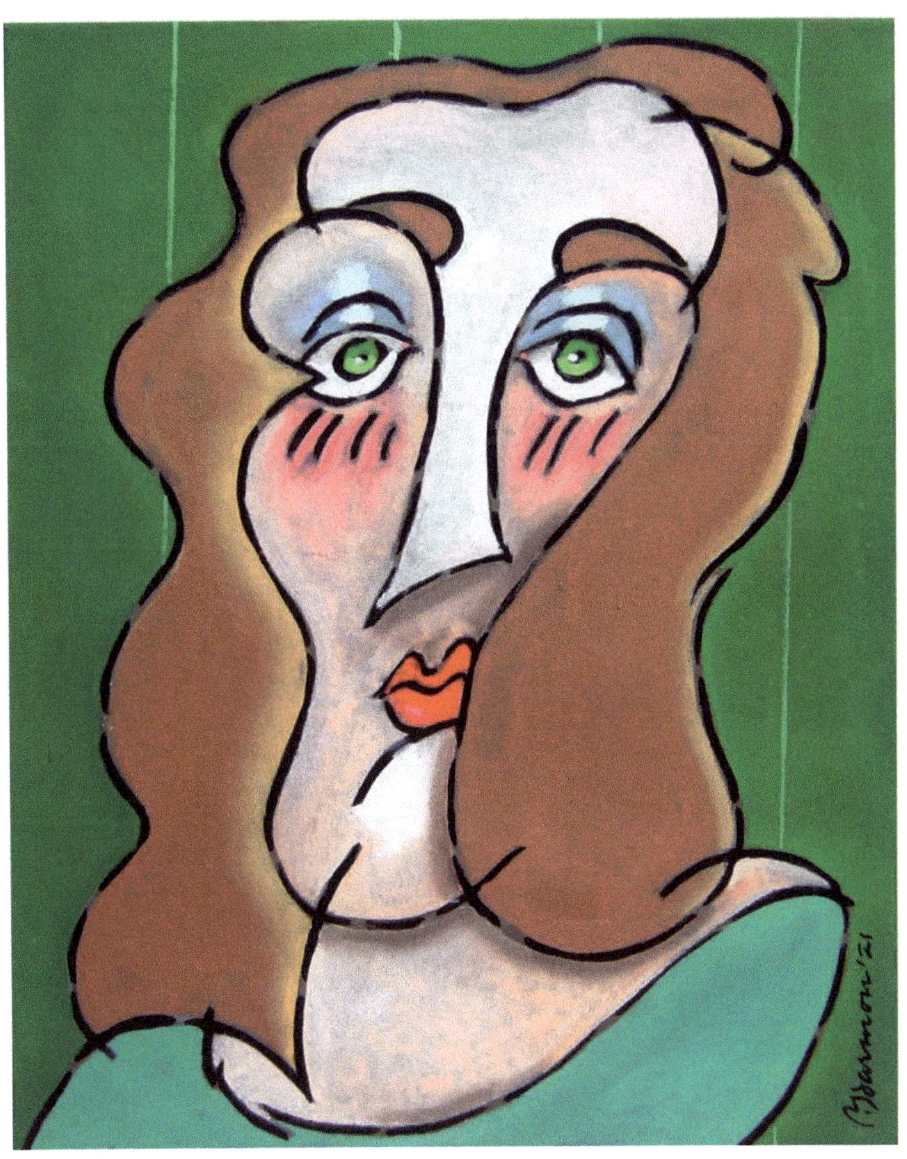

I find it easy to talk about my external world.
I can describe the workings, play by play.
My influences, my aims, and directions.
How simple and direct.
It is the inner world that is so difficult to put into words.
Perhaps impossible.
That is why I paint.
Painting is a language
Only slightly overlapped with words.

Paul Harmon

To solve a problem,
You begin to minimize its characteristics,
Diminish its importance,
Rob it of your attention,
Refuse it your energy.
The method is the opposite, of course,
Of what you are taught.
That is why it seems
To be so impractical.

Seth

Realize any idea that you accept as truth
Is a belief that you hold.
Questions you cannot seem to answer
As you study your own ideas,
For example
May lead you to suspect
The existence of invisible
Core beliefs.

Seth

Night Clouds Streaking Proud.
Moon's Half Lit.
Stars Act A Little Pissed.
Thunder Burps On Its Party's Shirt.
Red's In Trouble. Blue Missed A Double.
Constitutional Mess
Wears War On Its Vest.
Economic Grief. Abortion Beef.
Meat And Three Thief.
Beliefs Wear Briefs.
Below The Belt
On A Guarded Shelf.

HTM

Rain Clouds Know How
To Turn On The Spigot
And Get A Little Wicked.
Puddle Jumping In The Wind
Thoughts Trap Perceptions
In The Haze Of Sin.
Liberty Climbs. Beliefs Do Rhyme
When They Find Nature's Mind.
Like A Heavy Sweet Potato Rue.
Or Mushrooms Floating In A Dish Of Two.
Gut Busting Food
In Those Disco Shoes.
Just To Be Clear.
Nothing's Clear.

HTM

I look for the singular and unique voice.
A painting can be just as satisfying to the artist if it ends
With questions as opposed to answers.
My work is certainly composed of questions.
I don't think there are any answers.
I have never looked for answers in art.
It is enough and plenty to see glimpses
Of the human condition.

Paul Harmon

I was a tiny bug
Now a Mountain
I was left behind.
Now honored at the head.
You healed my wounded hunger
And anger,
And made me a poet
Who sings about joy.

Rumi

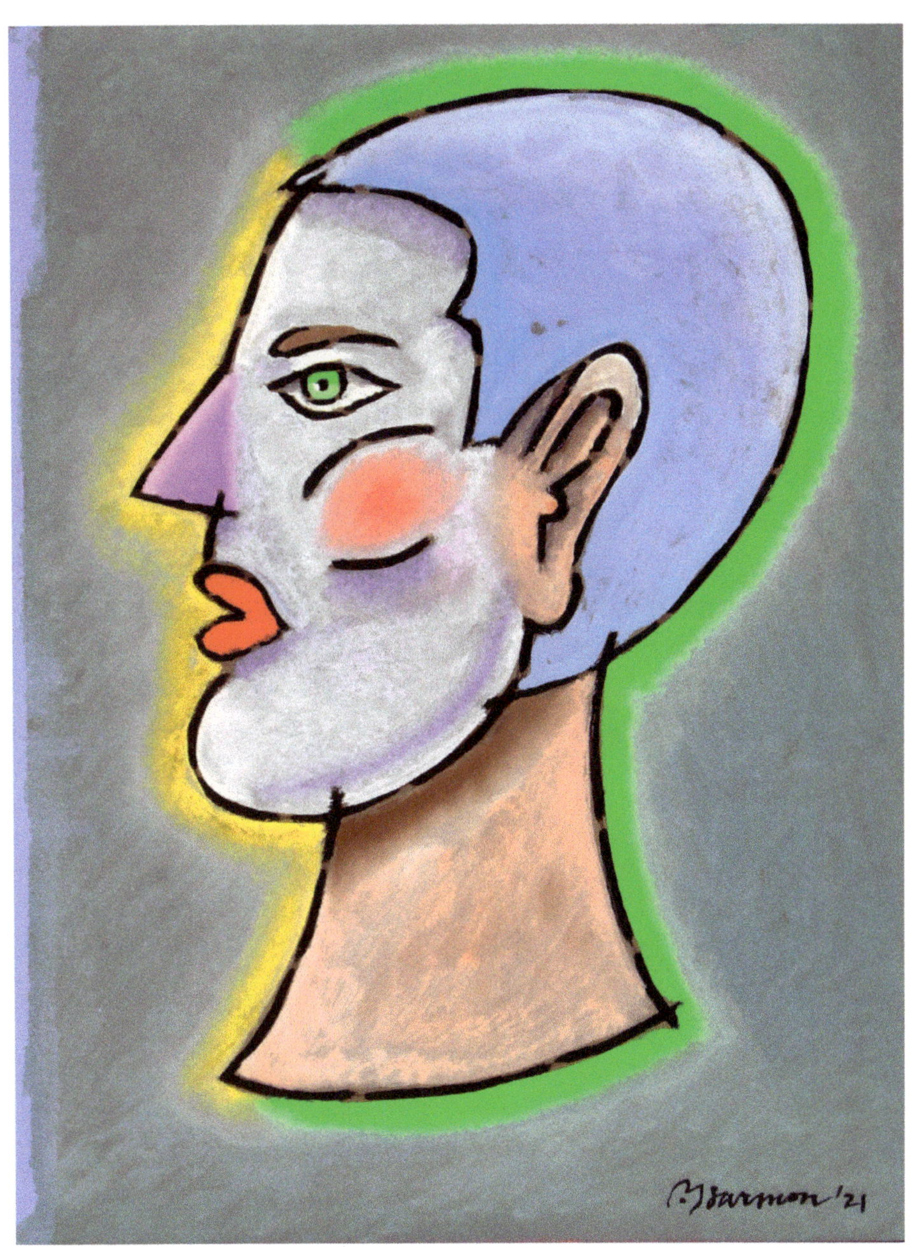

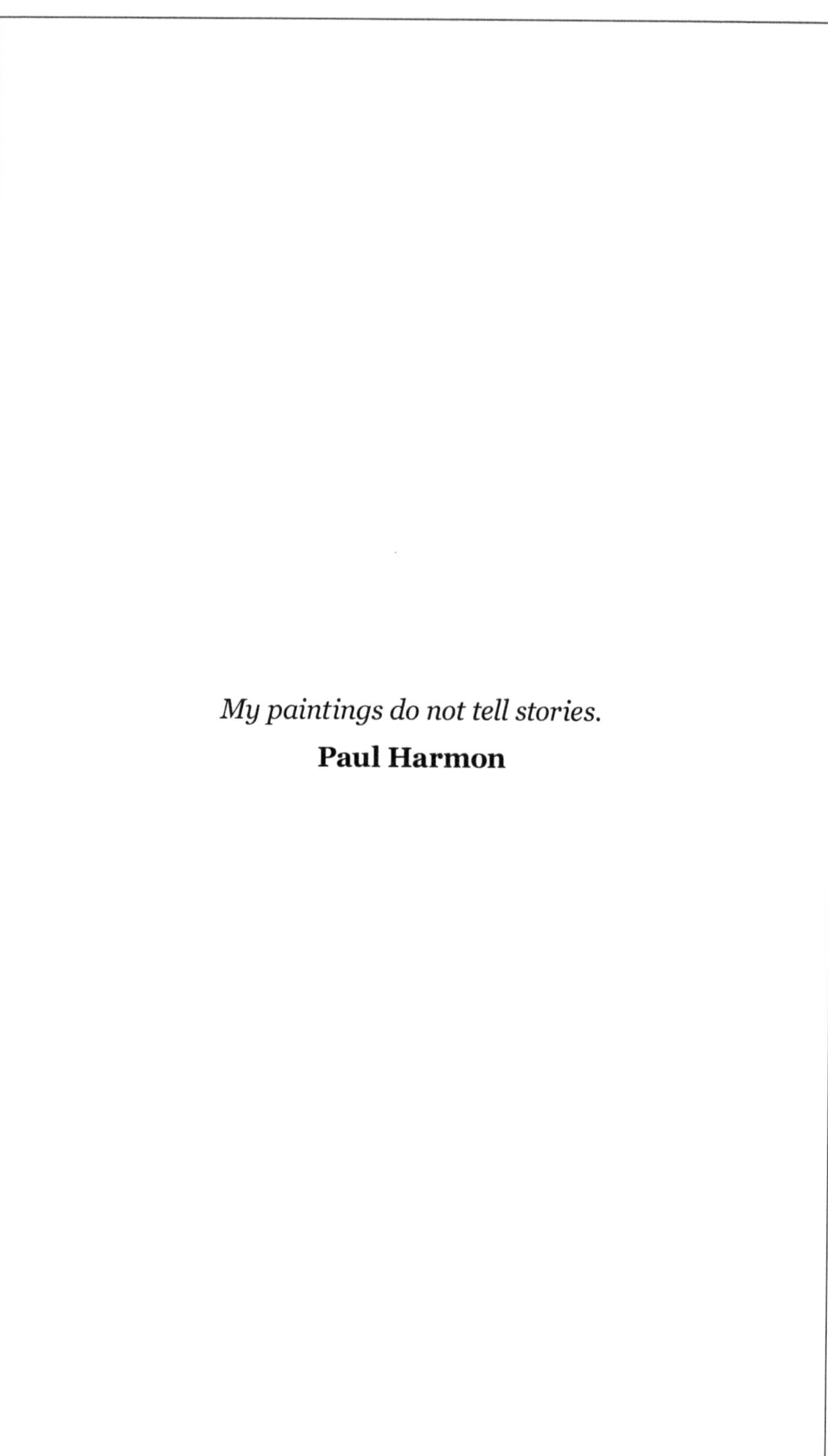

My paintings do not tell stories.

Paul Harmon

Hatred itself forms a very strong
Claim that will follow him throughout his lives,
Until he learns
That only the hatred itself is the destroyer.
I would like to make it clear
That there is nothing
To be gained, either,
By hating hatred.
You fall into the same trap.

Seth

Rabbit In The Rain
Running From Pain.
Stomach's Filled With Grass
Owls Chasing Ass.
It's A Big Top Show When Nature Knows
Crap Seems to Stick When Fear
Sticks Out That Upper Lip.
Walk With Me Around This Tree.
Branches Bare.
Shaped With Majestic Flair.
Leaves On The Ground Dance Around.
Green On Top Waits For The Flop.
Sitting Nest Rests At Squirrel's Request.
Chick-A-Dee Cries. Blue Jay Lies.
About The Loaf
Of Unleavened Toast
In A Speckled Egg Roast.

HTM

Art and Craft.
Craft without art
Is a dry and soulless thing.
Art without craft is a shambles.
It is all about the right balance.

Paul Harmon

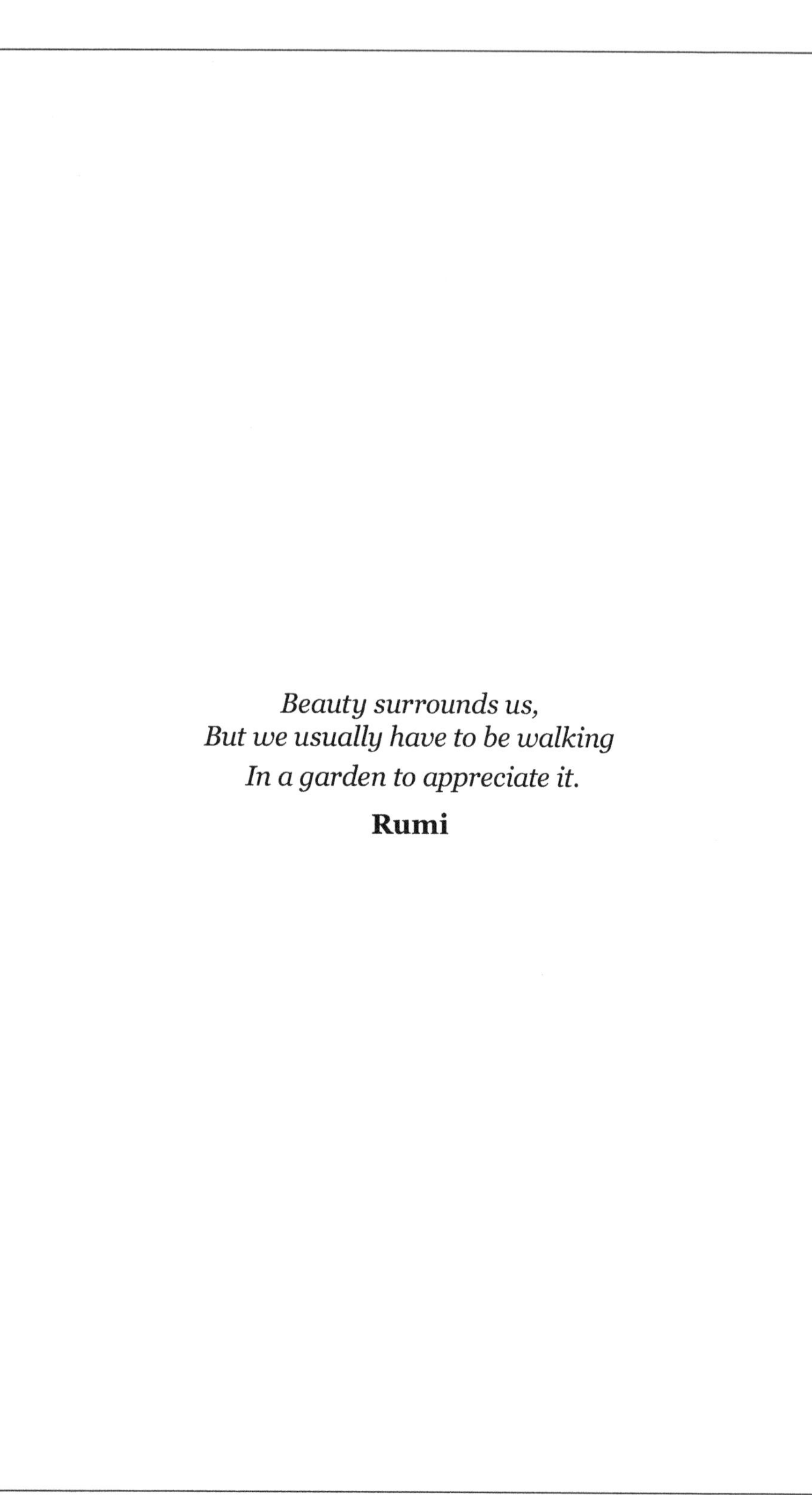

Beauty surrounds us,
But we usually have to be walking
In a garden to appreciate it.

Rumi

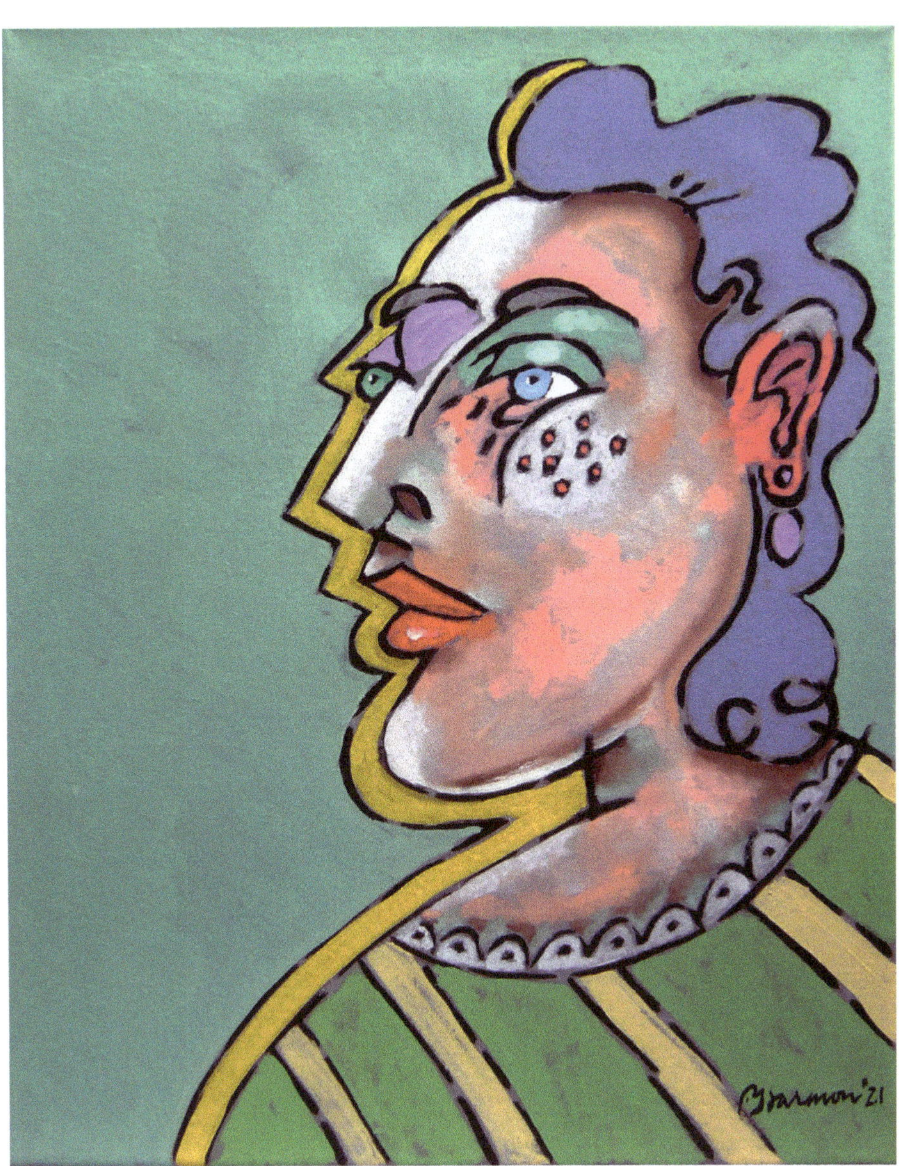
Harmon'21

Your beliefs
Automatically attract the appropriate emotions.
They reinforce themselves through imagination;
And at the risk of repeating myself,
Because this is so important:
Imagination and feeling follow your Beliefs.
It is not the other way around.

Seth

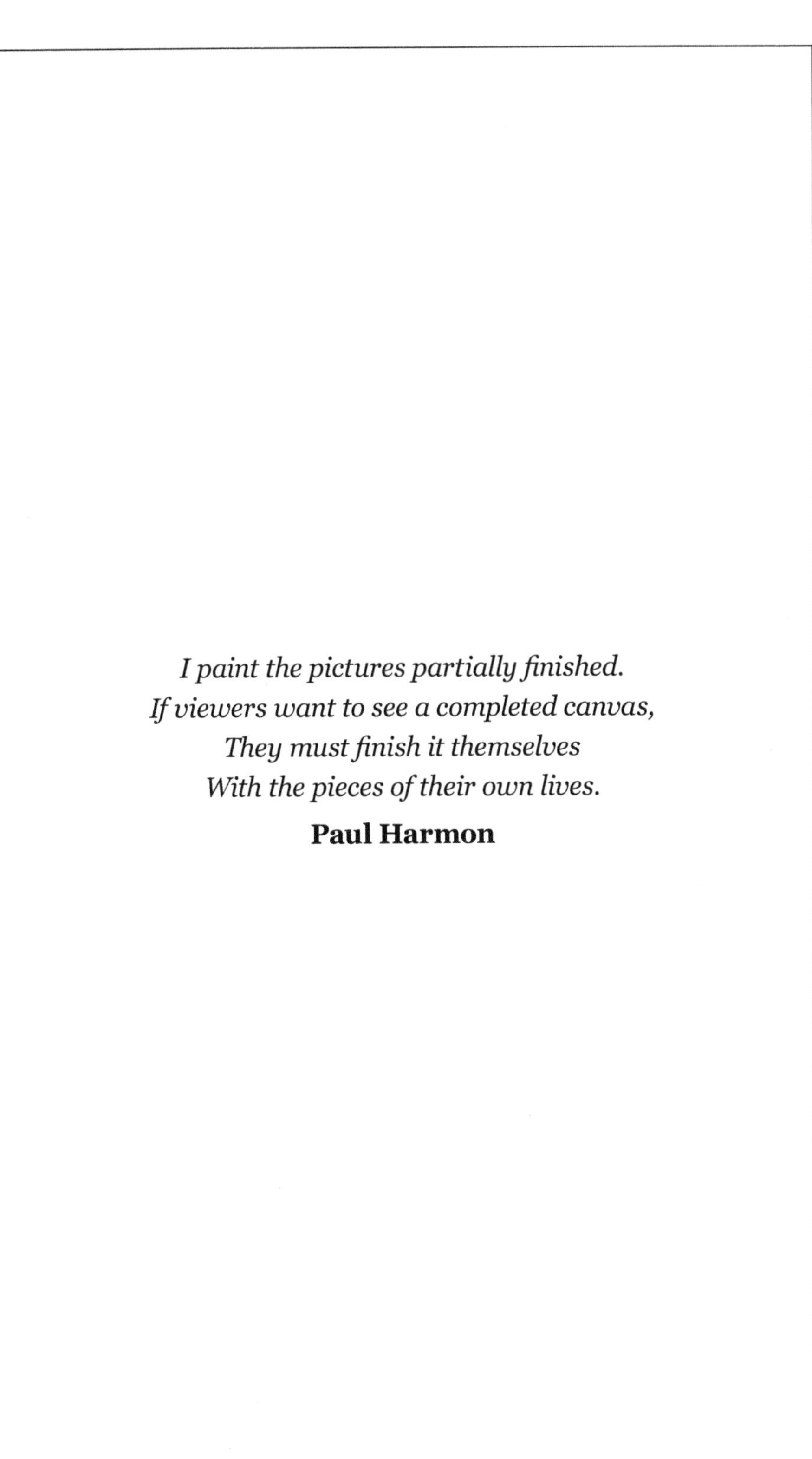

I paint the pictures partially finished.
If viewers want to see a completed canvas,
They must finish it themselves
With the pieces of their own lives.

Paul Harmon

Angel Bird What's The Word?
Pacman Moon? Baby Bunny Shoes?
Capitalistic Ghouls Opened A Cesspool.
Easy Swim If You're In.
Ignorance Flies At The Feet Of Lies.
White-Laced Mess Same Old Quest.
Beliefs Sink Low Just To Show
Diversity's Glow.

HTM

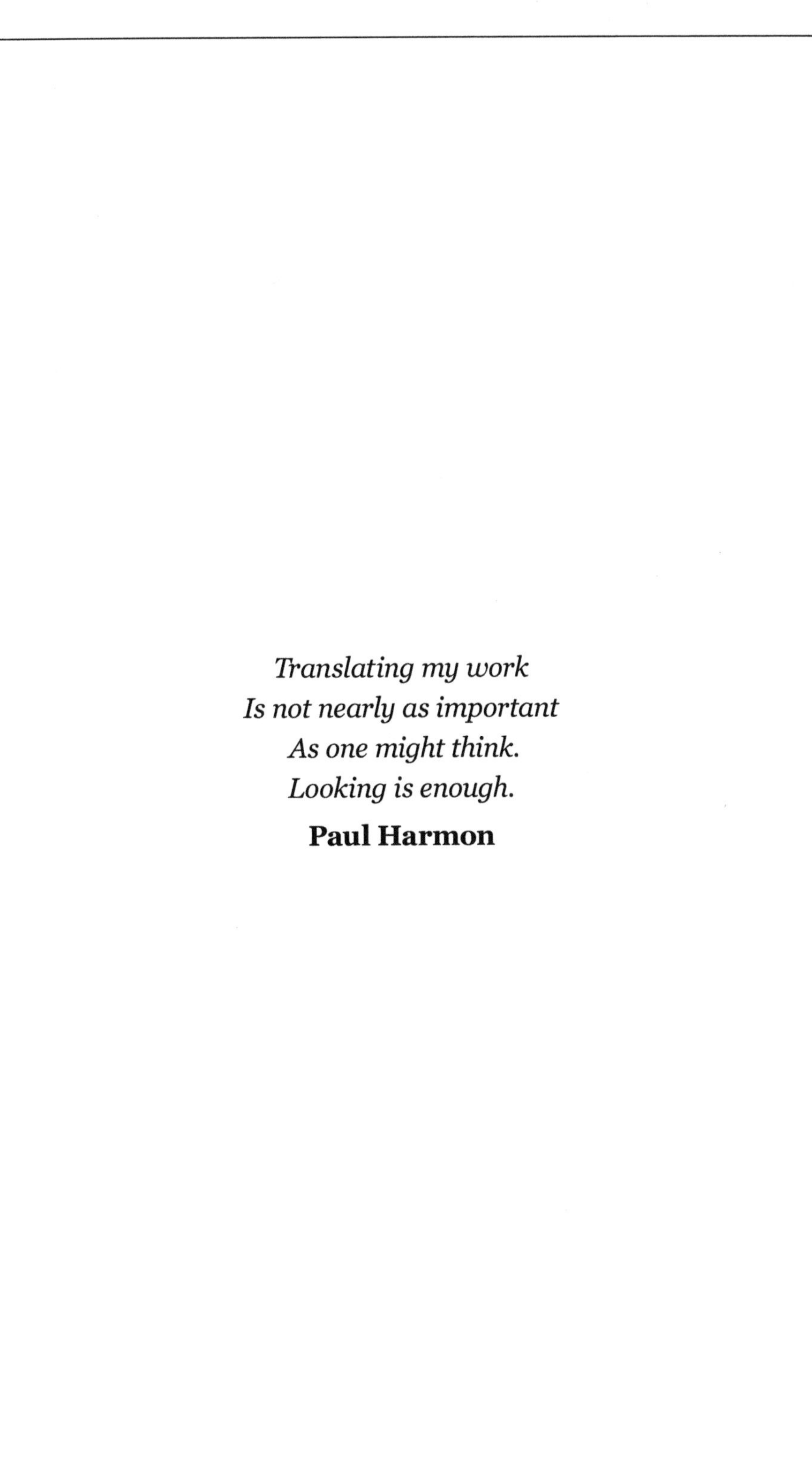

Translating my work
Is not nearly as important
As one might think.
Looking is enough.

Paul Harmon

It's the old rule
That drunks have to argue
And get into fights.
The lover is just as bad.
He falls into a hole.
But down in that hole
He finds something shining,
Worth more than any amount
Of money or power.

Rumi

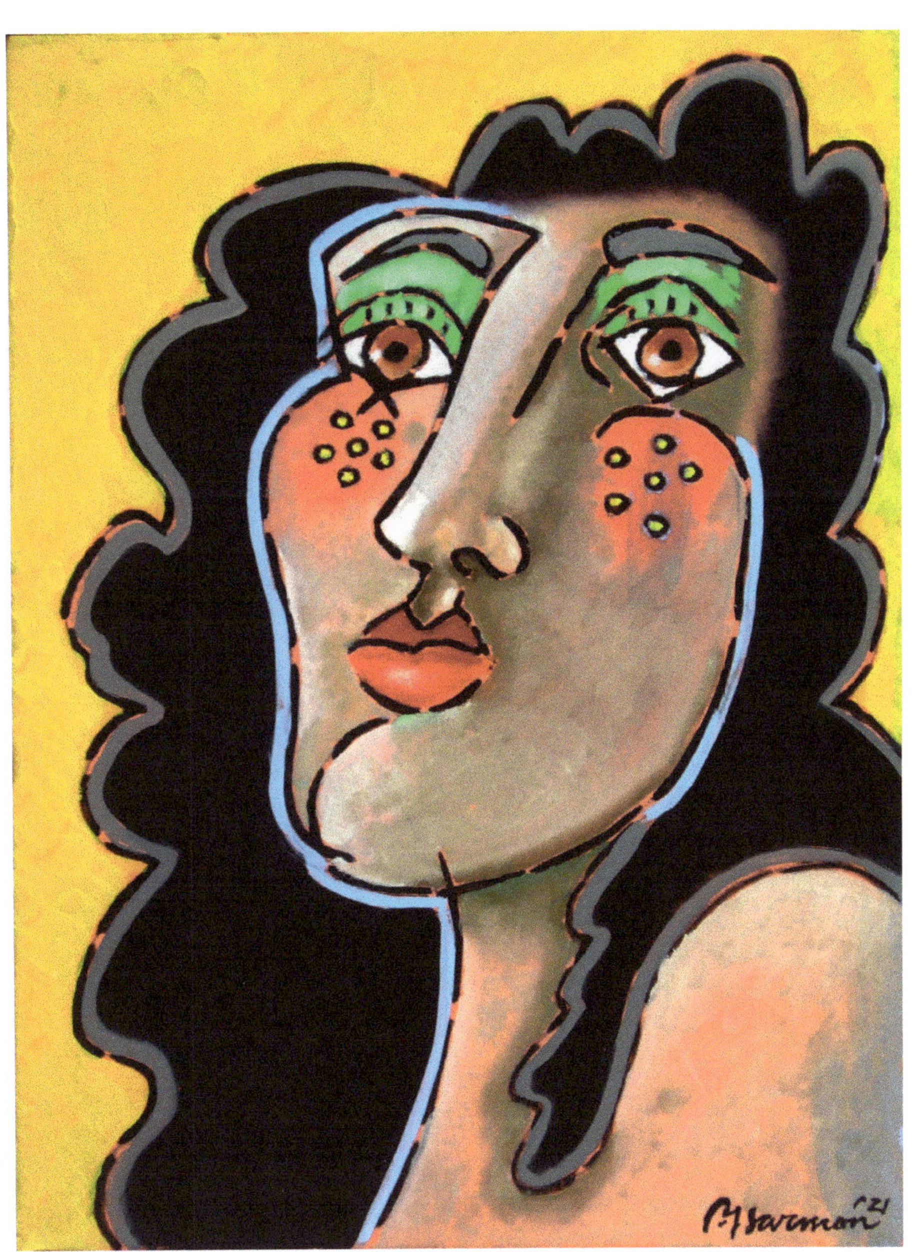

I am not interested
In painting a picture of something.
It is the thinking
That goes along with the process
Of painting
That is so seductive.
Like seeing
The other side of the moon.

Paul Harmon

Pop Can In The Middle Of The Road
Nerves About To Explode
Planet's Got Fuzz Up Its Nose
Fear And Love
Take Off The Gloves
One Stirs Hate
The Other's Soft-Baked
Into The Lives Of Mankind.
Travel To Your Inner Room
Leave The Gloom
On A Mental Laundry Spoon.
Stars Are There.
Freedom Runs In Pairs
Without A Fare.

HTM

Your systems of belief
Will of course attract certain kinds of thoughts,
With their trails of emotional experience.
A steady barrage of hateful,
Revengeful thoughts should actually
Lead you
To look for the beliefs
From which they are gaining their strength.
Belief systems are as necessary
And natural as physical organs are.
In fact, their purpose is to help you direct
The functioning of your biological being.

Seth

Blanket Of Dreams Frazzled Seams.
Bags Of Noise Filled With Ancient Toys.
Temperature's Hot In Earth's Sweet Spot.
What's The Bet When Wind Drives A Jet?
What's The Score When Anger
Beats Down A Golden Door?
High Tide Swim. Without Fins.
Weather's In A Changing Jar.
Thoughts Drink At A Foggy Bar.
Who Scores The Goal When Truth
Fits In A Black Hole?

HTM

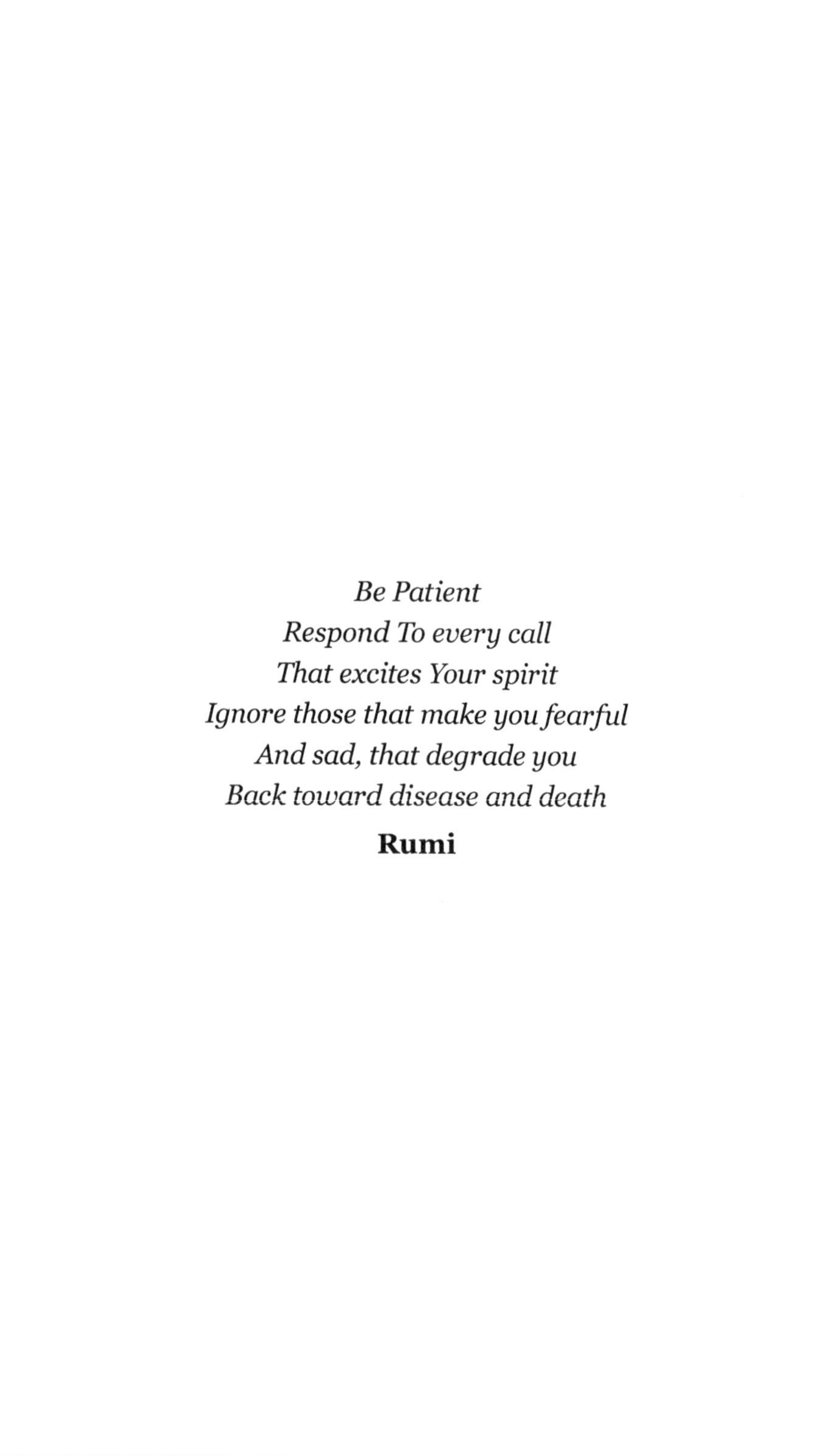

Be Patient
Respond To every call
That excites Your spirit
Ignore those that make you fearful
And sad, that degrade you
Back toward disease and death

Rumi

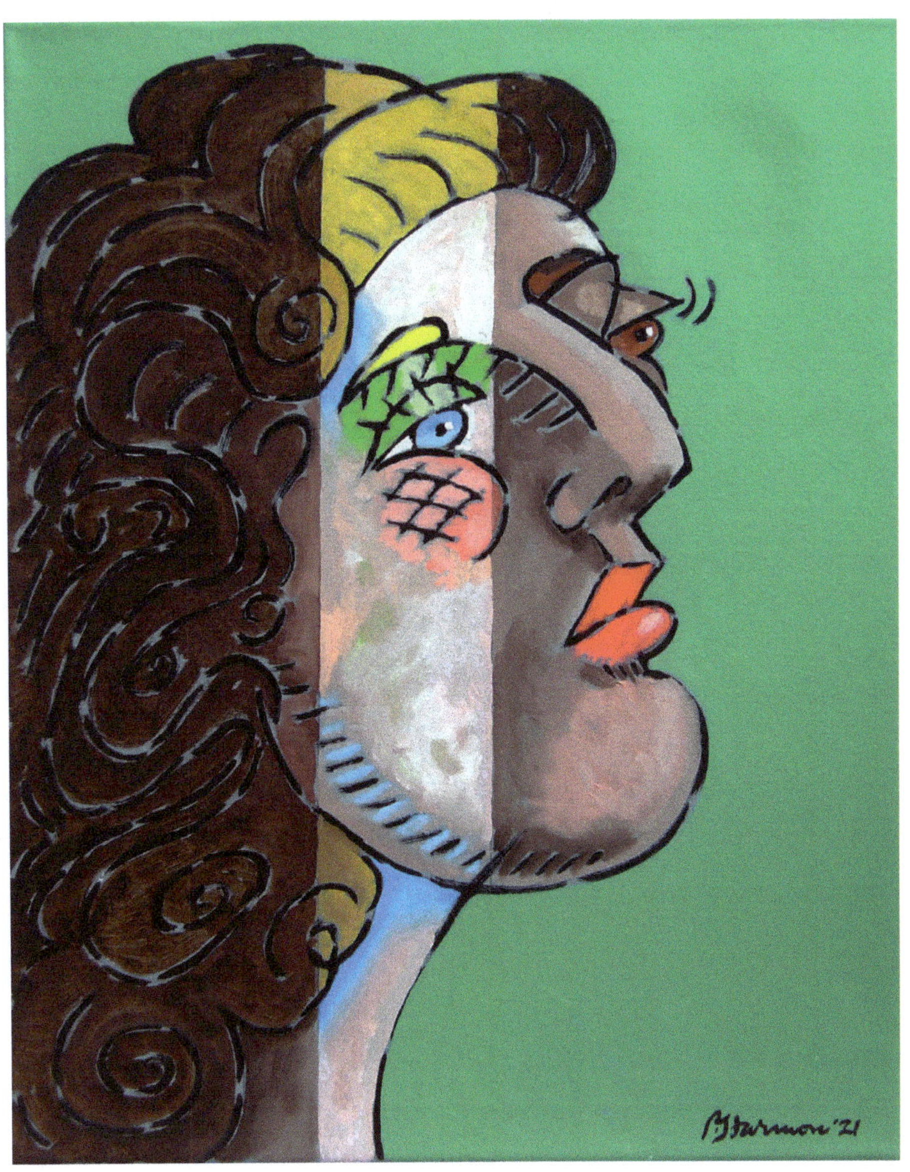

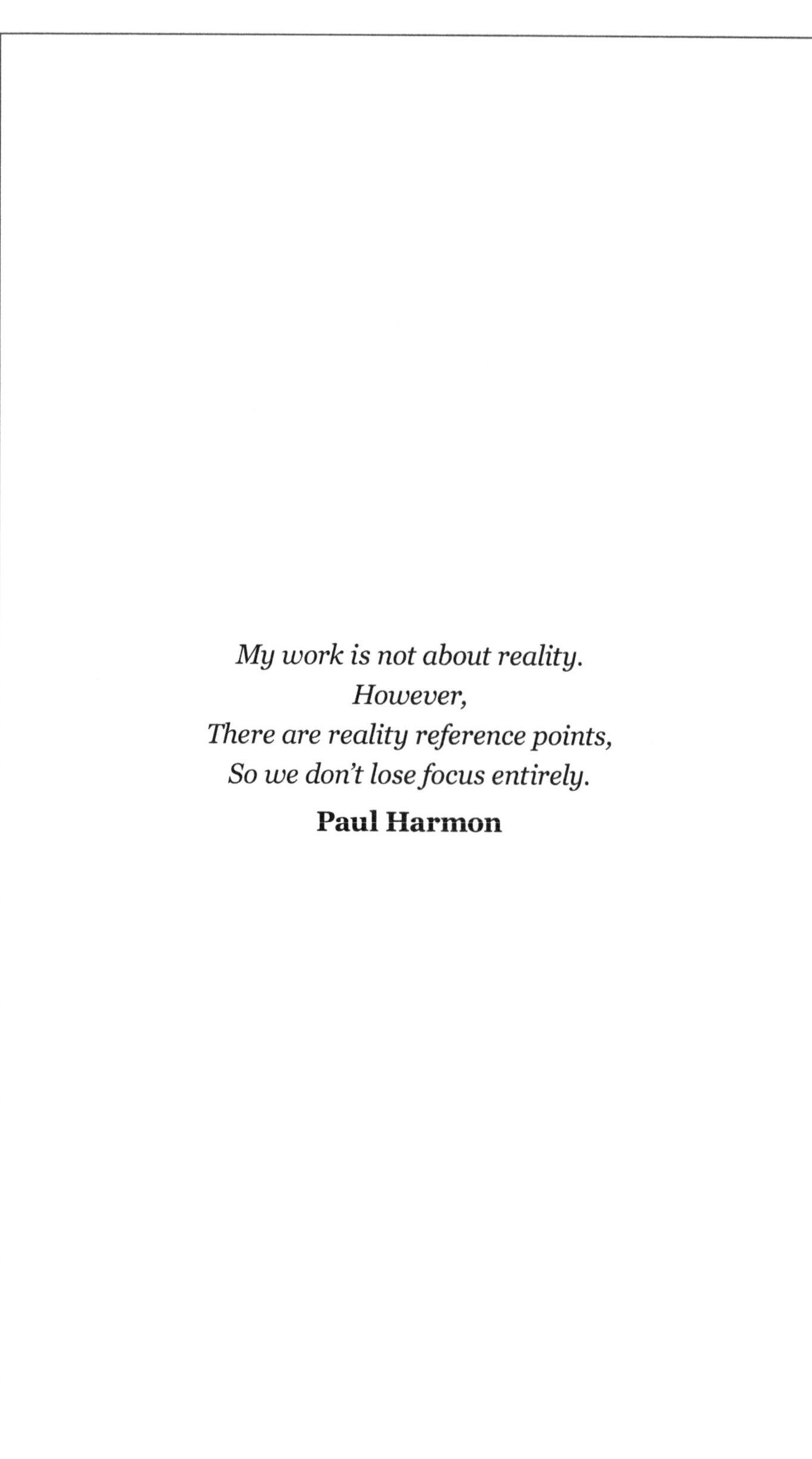

My work is not about reality.
However,
There are reality reference points,
So we don't lose focus entirely.

Paul Harmon

There is a kind of innate gallantry
That operates among all segments of life —
A gallantry
That deserves your respect and consideration.
You should have respect, then,
For the cells of your body,
The thoughts of your mind,
And try to understand
Even the smallest of creatures
Shares with you
The emotional experience
Of life's triumphs
And vulnerabilities.

Seth

Secret Garden Thoughts Like To Bargain
In The Mist Of Ancient Myths.
School Bus Gold Starts To Erode
Awareness Implodes
On A Beach Where Guns Meet.
Sideway Chirps Massive Blurbs
Truth Slurps. Time Burps.
In A Dish Of Killer Pain.
Unless You Claim
That Inner You
Who Sticks Like Glue
To All That's True.

HTM

The use of talent and craft
To "make pictures"
Is not what I look for.
I look for the singular and unique voice.
Curious, how something
Odd and new
And abrasive best shows
The spirt of man
And life on the planet.

Paul Harmon

Say something new!
It is wonderful to move
To a new place every day.
It is wonderful to flow
Without ice and mud
Everything my friends,
Is gone with yesterday.
All the words are gone.
Now is the time
To say something new.

Rumi

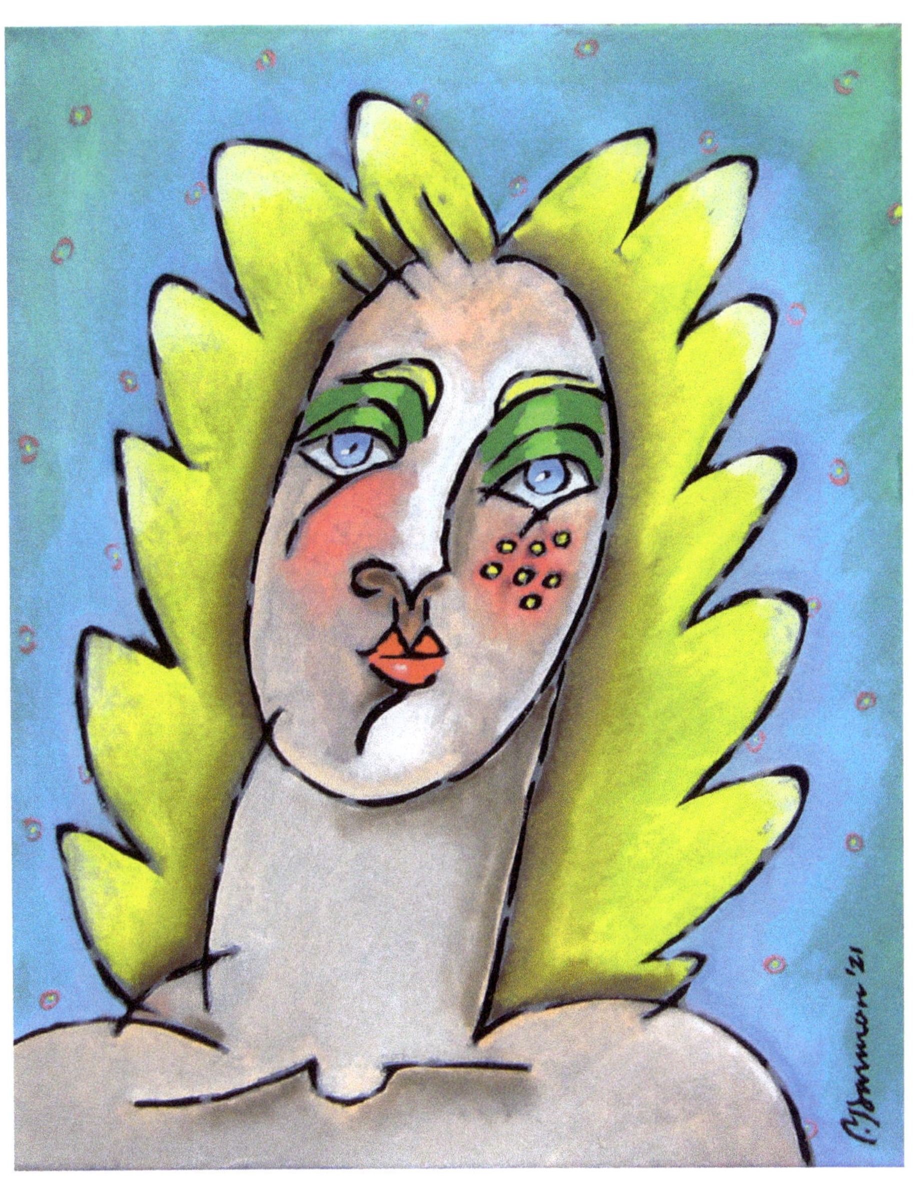

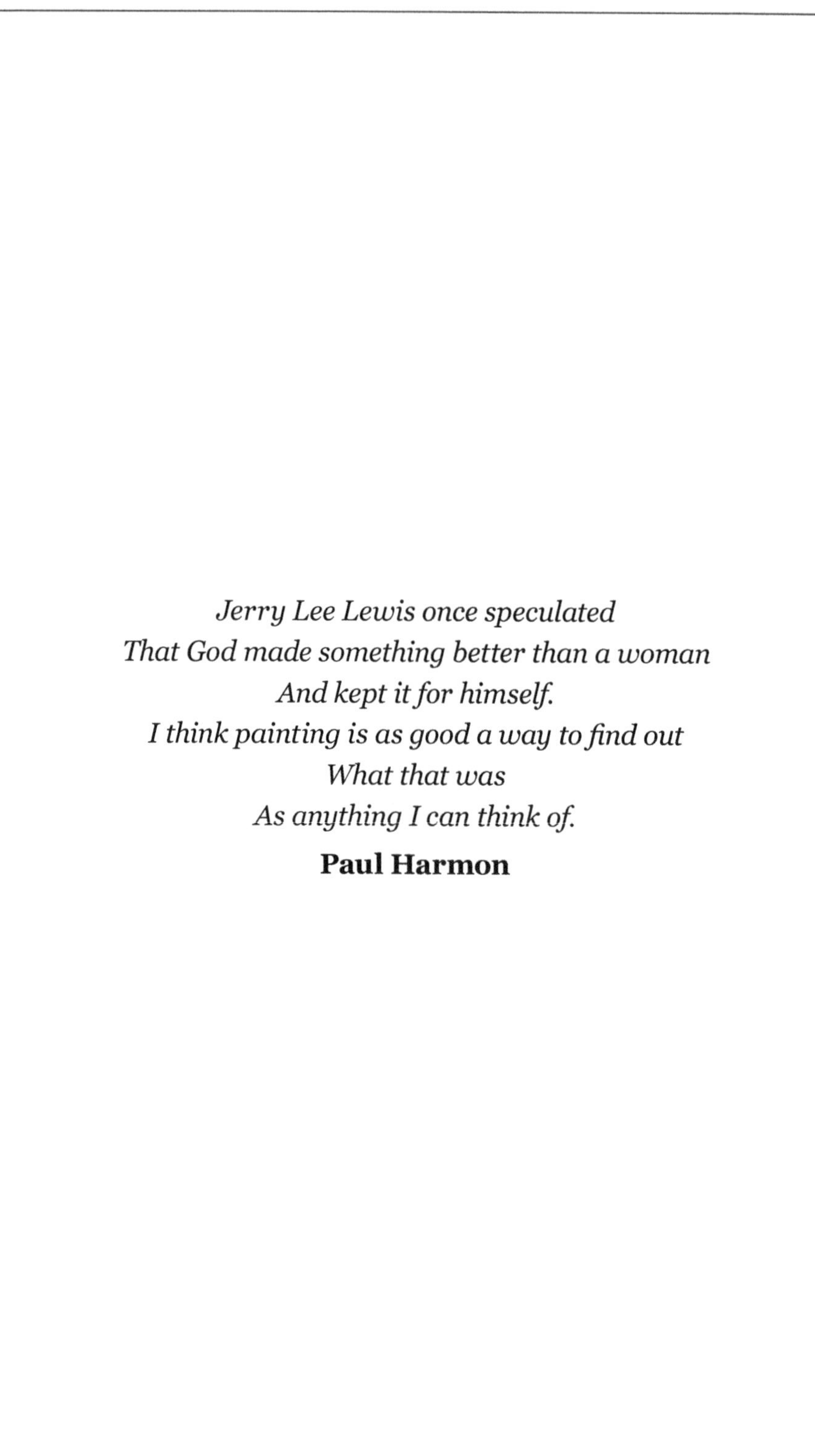

Jerry Lee Lewis once speculated
That God made something better than a woman
And kept it for himself.
I think painting is as good a way to find out
What that was
As anything I can think of.

Paul Harmon

Two Black Eyes. Trust Flies By.
Self-Defeating Lies. King Of The Flies.
Nothing Sits Tight
When Anger Takes Flight.
Take Off The Gloves There Are No Flubs.
Choices Reign In A Sea Of Pain.
Thoughts Act In A Soul Contract.
What You Seek Is Your Heart Beat.
Cells Divide. God's On The Ride.
Allies And Foes Filter Through
The Human Soul.
Core Beliefs Are Special Treats
They Build The Road
Choices Go.

HTM

Imagination
Also plays an important part
In your subjective life,
As it gives mobility to your beliefs.
It is one of the motivating agencies
That helps transform your beliefs
Into physical experience.
It is vital
You understand the interrelationship
Between ideas and imagination.
In order to dislodge unsuitable beliefs
And establish new ones,
You must learn to use your imagination
To move concepts in and out of your mind.
"The proper use of imagination
Can then propel ideas
In the directions you desire.

Seth

I can't work with only the facts
Of life around me.
I must add dreams to the mix
To capture the essence
Of this being human
On Earth.

Paul Harmon

Love has taken away my practices
And filled me with poetry.
I tried to keep quietly repeating,
No strength but yours,
But I couldn't.
I had to clap and sing.
I used to be respectable
And chaste and stable,
But who can stand in this strong wind
And remember those things?
A mountain keeps an echo deep inside itself.
That's how I hold your voice.

Rumi

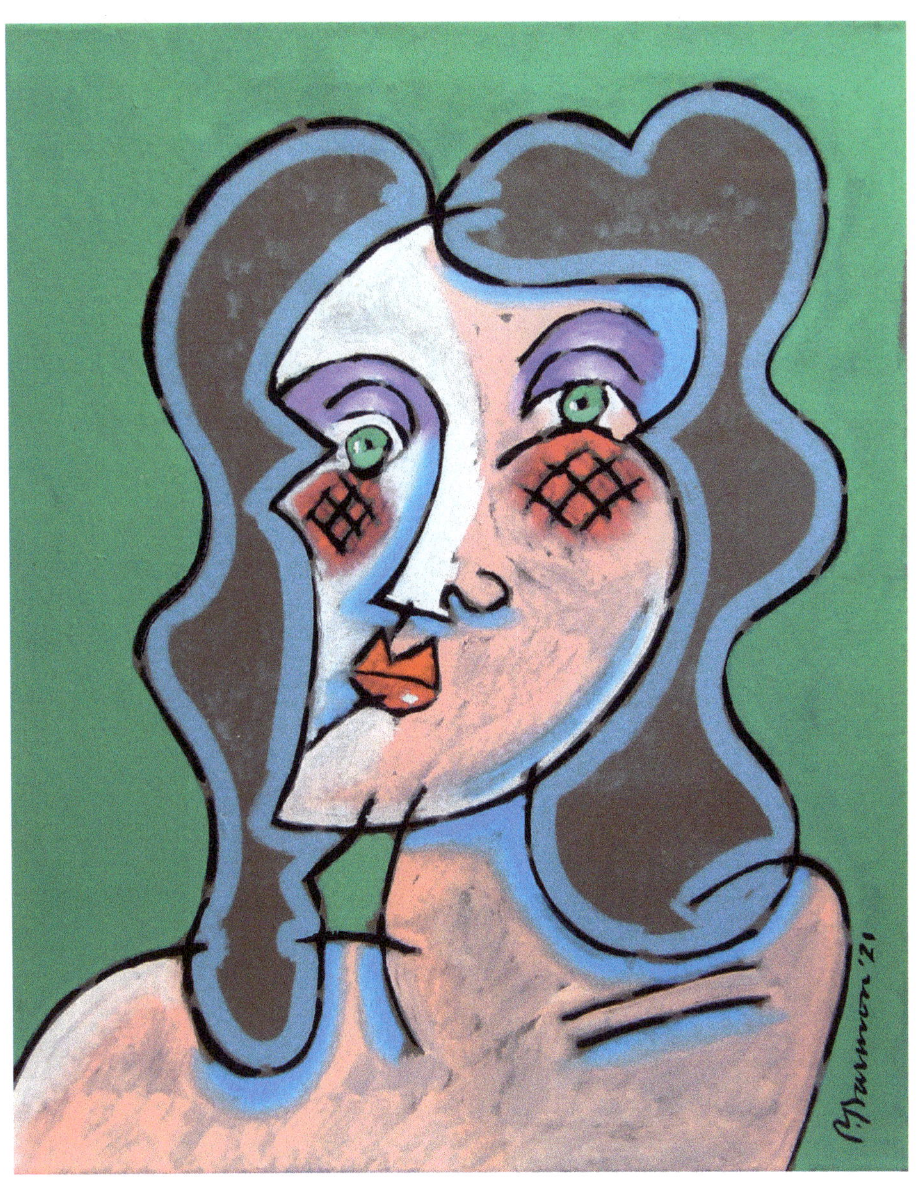

If you believe that you are a beast
And no better than a beast
And you have a poor opinion of beasts,
[then] Indeed you will find self-love a horrendous barrier.

If you understand the beauty
And miracle and spirituality of your flesh
And of any beast or the smallest fly or ant,
Then self-love becomes a benediction
That the universe gives you

And that you,
As a portion of the universe,
Give yourself.

Seth

It's the most frustrating and exciting thing
I can think of to do in life.
It's like looking in a mirror.
I like to see graphically
What's going on
In my mind.

Paul Harmon

Rip One Off Let's Get Loud
Awareness Wears A Scently Crown.
Conch Shell White. God's In Sight.
Ring That Chime Hummingbird Time.
Beauty's Fan Sits On A Stand.
Eagle Grins. Wings Don't Sin.
Wafer Thin Win.
In The Backseat Of A Crowd
You Gotta Know How.

HTM

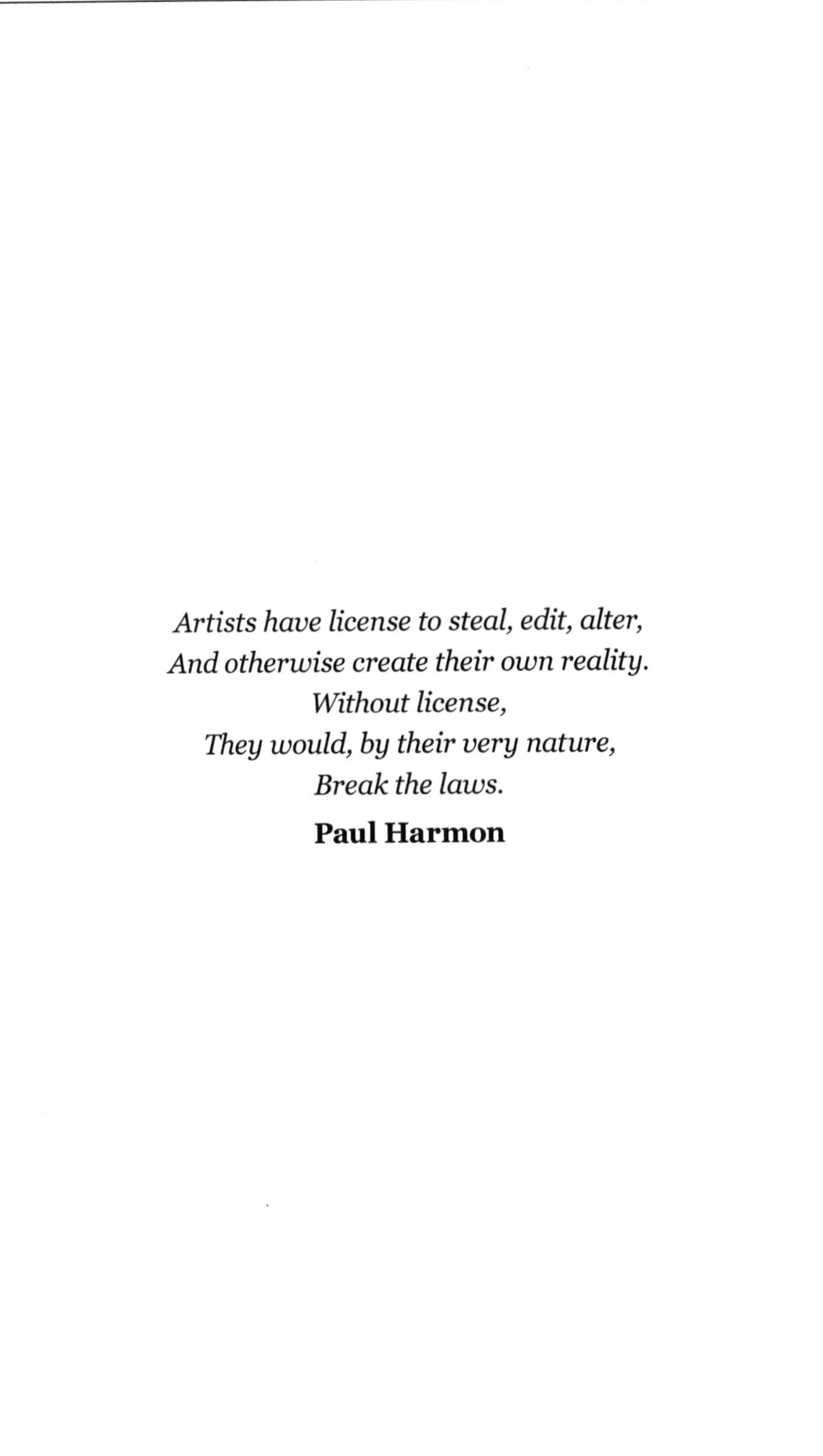

Artists have license to steal, edit, alter,
And otherwise create their own reality.
Without license,
They would, by their very nature,
Break the laws.

Paul Harmon

We have fallen into a place
Where everything is music
The strumming
And the flute notes
Rise into the atmosphere,
And even if the whole world's harp
Should burn up,
There will still be hidden
Instruments playing.

Rumi

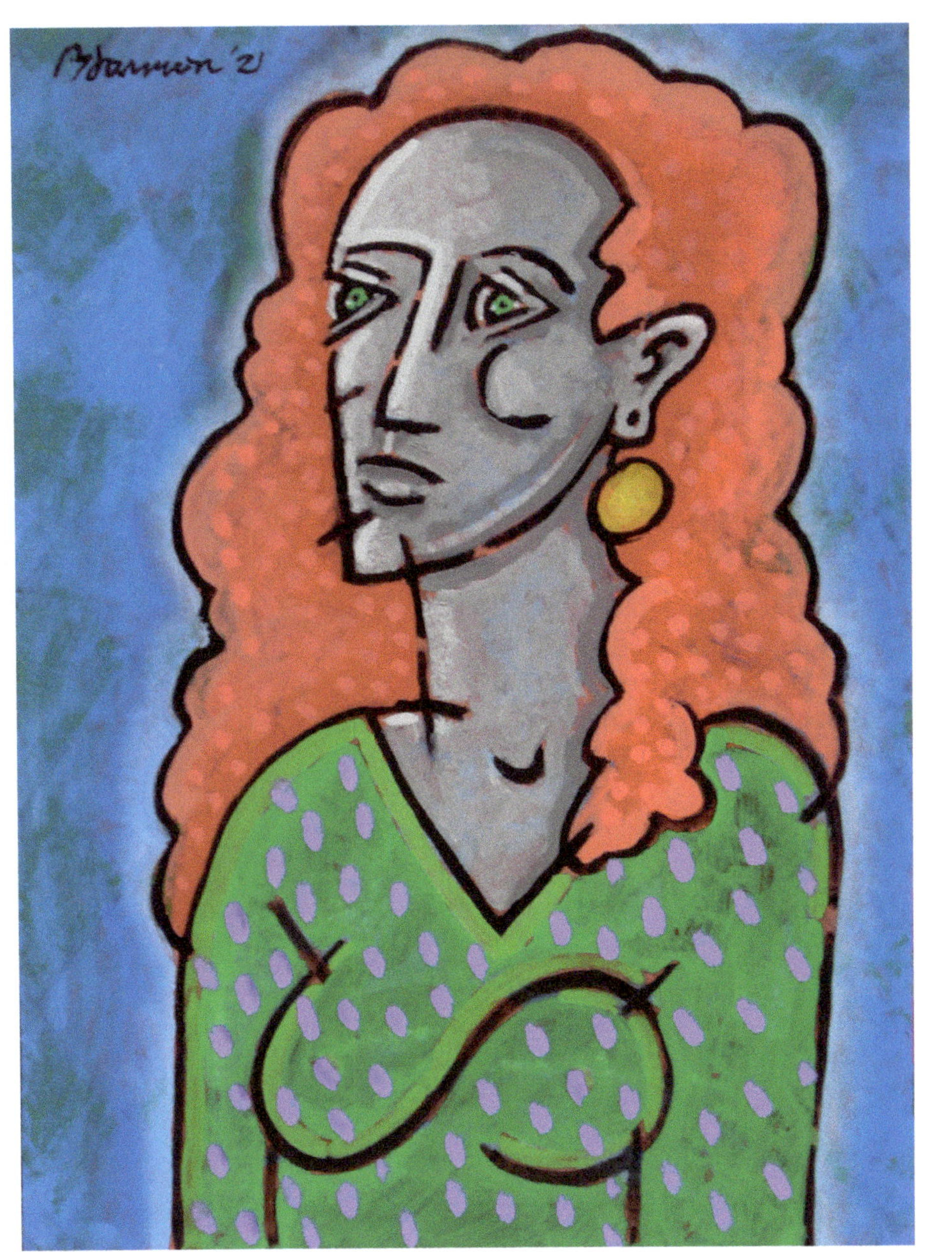

Largely, but not completely,
Your imagination follows your beliefs,
As do your emotions.
One of the most hampering beliefs of all
Is the idea that the clues to current behavior
Are buried and usually inaccessible.
This belief itself closes to you the contents
Of your own conscious mind
And prevents you from looking
There for the answers
That are available.

Seth

Sugar Drop Tree
Enlighten Me
Emerging Trends
Thoughts That Bend
Reality's Motion Is
Like A Fine-Tuned String
Of Dancing Things.
Bible Growls. Jesus Howls.
Buddha Had A Lot Of Towels.
On The Prowl For A Dance
To The Music
Deep Inside His
Tree Of Now.

HTM

Each of you automatically
Heal yourselves day by day,
Cells die
And you are being taught,
And you are teaching yourselves
To handle energy,
To become conscious co-creators
With All That Is,
And one of the 'stages of development'
Or learning processes includes
Dealing with opposites as realities.

In your terms, the ideas of good and evil
Help you recognize
The sacredness of existence,
The responsibility of consciousness
Born.

You renew your bodies
Every seven years,
All without your conscious knowledge.
You use the energy of the universe
To heal yourselves constantly,
But you have very definite conclusion
As what's possible
And what is not possible.

Seth

Fishing Tools Don't Be Cruel
Shifting Poles Truth Be Told
Do The Flip When Consciousness Rolls
In Frozen Lakes
In The Land That Quakes.
Scales Of Fear Beliefs Draw Near.
Perceptions Find A Pier
That Holds Thoughts A Little Taunt
While Imagination Plays Truth Or Dare
In A Bucket Of Hot Air.

HTM

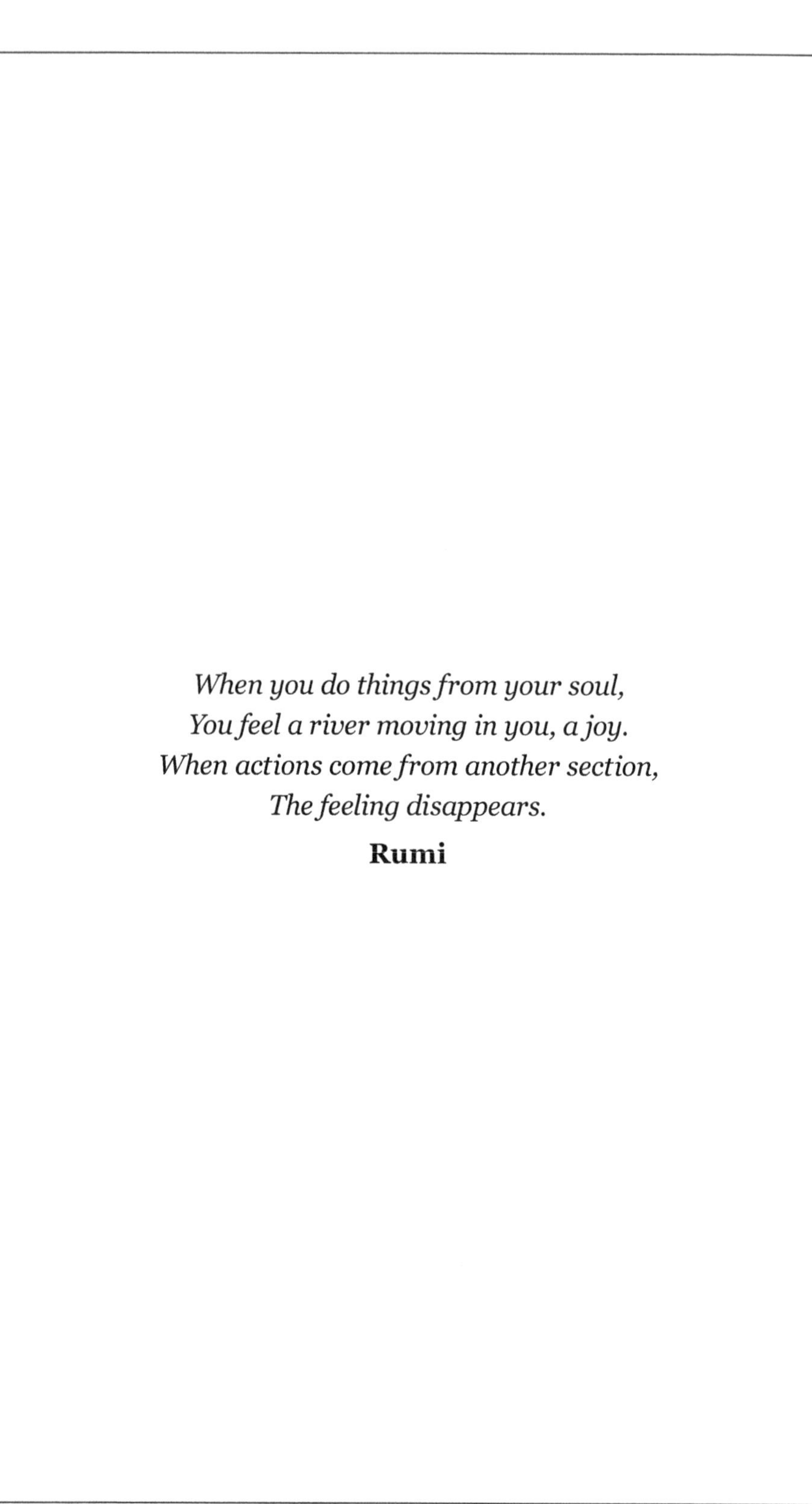

When you do things from your soul,
You feel a river moving in you, a joy.
When actions come from another section,
The feeling disappears.

Rumi

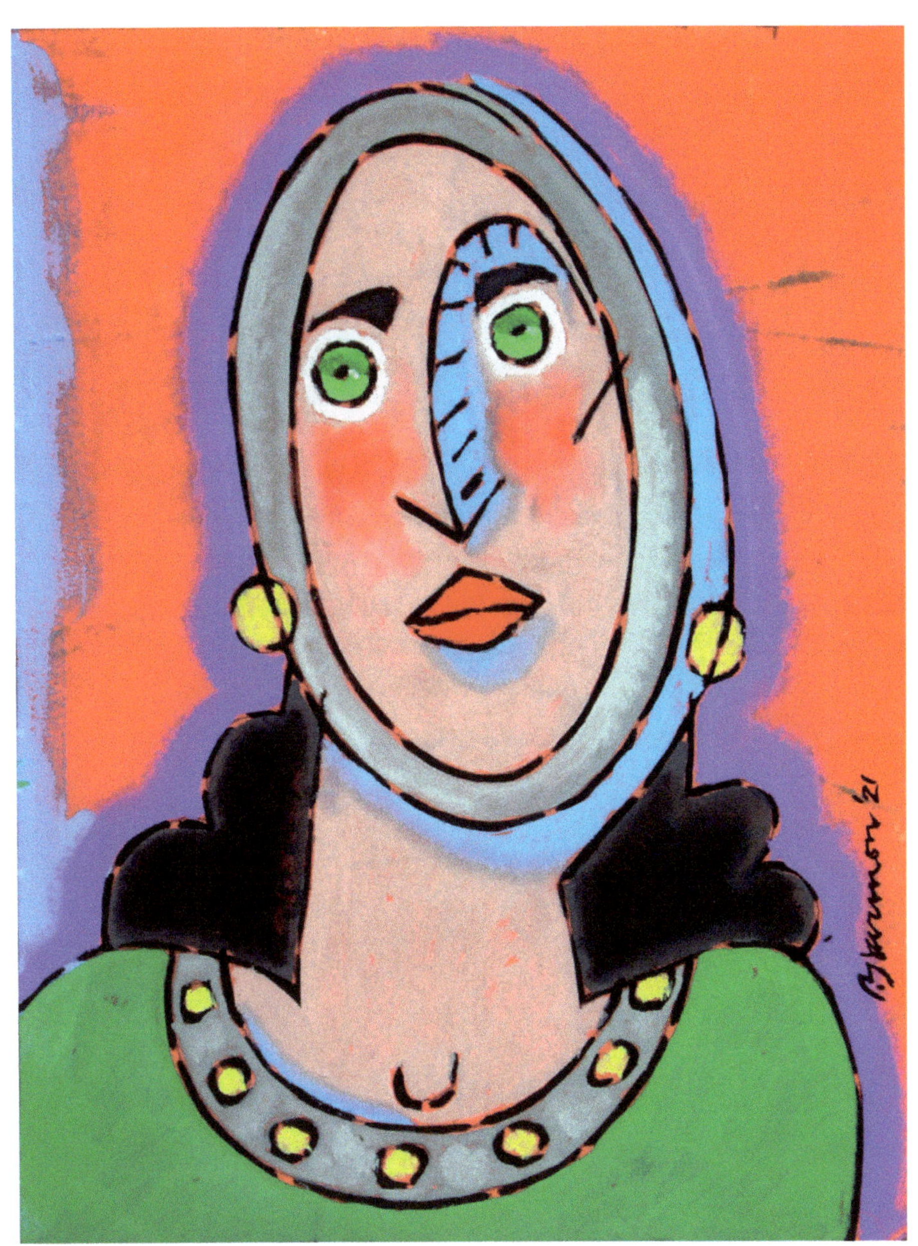

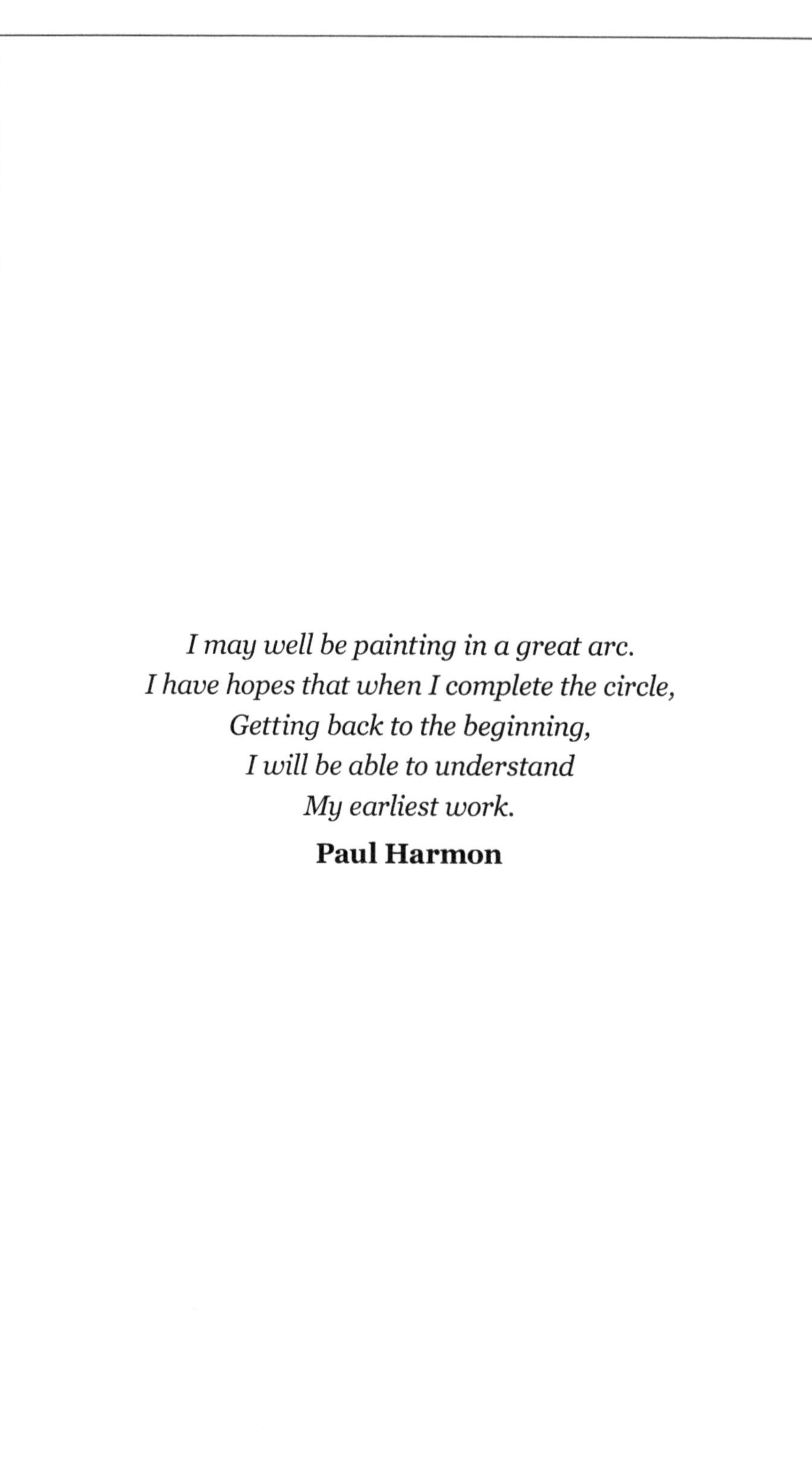

I may well be painting in a great arc.
I have hopes that when I complete the circle,
Getting back to the beginning,
I will be able to understand
My earliest work.

Paul Harmon

Your thoughts form structures
As real as the cells.
Their composition is different
In that no solidity is involved in your terms.
As living cells have a structure,
React to stimuli
And organize according
To their own classification,
So do thoughts.
Thoughts thrive on association.
They magnetically attract others like themselves,
And like some strange microscopic animals
They repel their 'enemies,'
Or other thoughts that are threatening
To their own survival.

Seth

I never want any of my remarks
To be construed in such a fashion
That it seems I am in any way negating the fullness,
Validity, and magnificence of physical existence.
I do want to point out, however,
That a state you usually call dreaming
Is but a dim indication of an inner reality of events,
An inner order of events
From which the physical world emerges.

Seth

I am aware that I am struggling against the wind,
Against all manner of cosmic forces,
To find something that is unfindable. . .

Don Quixote at windmills or perhaps a better analogy,
Hamlet, in a high drama that is ultimately about nothing.
But, oh, the beauty of the adventure.

Paul Harmon

This is love:
To fly toward a secret sky,
To cause a hundred veils
To fall each moment
First, to let go of life.
In the end, to take a step without feet.
To regard this world as invisible,
And to disregard what appears to the self.

Rumi

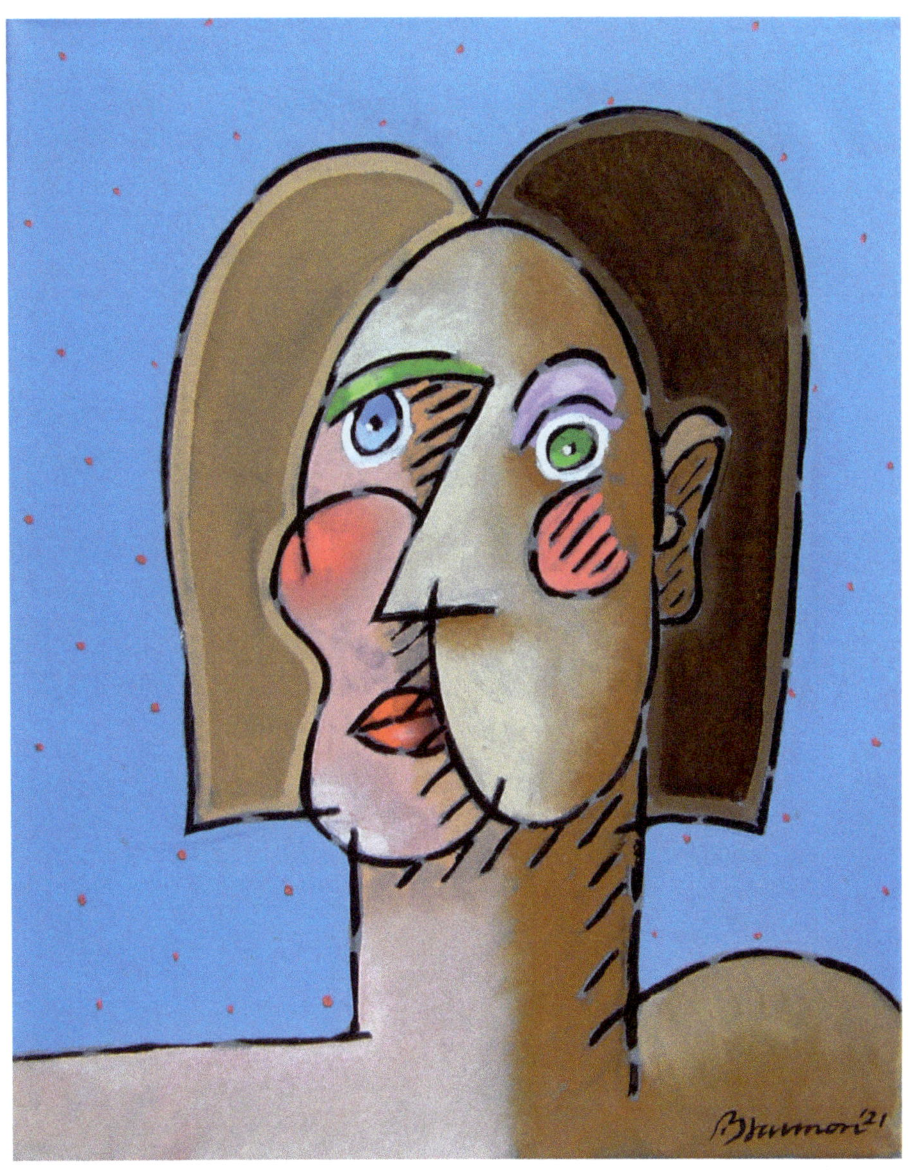

Top Of The World Begins To Curl
Old Images Sink In The Deep.
Perception Haze Thoughts Seem Dazed.
Run With The Ball Life's Your Mall.
Purchase A Ticket Dreams Comes With It.
Moments Release Dressed With Peace.
Facial Stand's Looking Grand.
Marbles On The Table Forget The Fables.
Need Help Touching That Inner Self
When Fear Roars
At The Sound Of A Door?
Grab A Belief By Its Pores
And Score.

HTM

You must become aware of your own structures.
Build them up or tear them down,
But do not allow yourself to become blind
To the furniture of your own mind...
It will help you, in fact,
If you think of your own beliefs
As furniture that can be rearranged,
Changed, renewed,
Completely discarded or replaced.
Your ideas are yours.
They should not control you...
Imagine yourself then rearranging this furniture.
Images of particular pieces
Will come clearly to you.

Seth

Who Are You Now?
That Face In The Crowd?
God On A Stick? Wandering Dick?
You Got Stoned And Not Alone.
You're A Prancer With All The Answers.
Excuse Shaker Who's Your Baker?
On A Roll Of Self-Made Woes.
You Like To Scream When Fear's Your Team.
Frozen Thoughts Cross The Line
Morality Time.
Spread The Bread. Forget The Lead.
You're Not What You Eat.
But You Are What You Think.

HTM

I find that I have developed
Or uncovered a pictorial sense
In that certain forms are compatible
With rhythms within me.
These forms, gestures, hues, and punctuations
Are always
Ready to debate the codes of representation
I have inherited from dead painters.
I owe these artists much,
And they are deeply submersed
In my work.

Paul Harmon

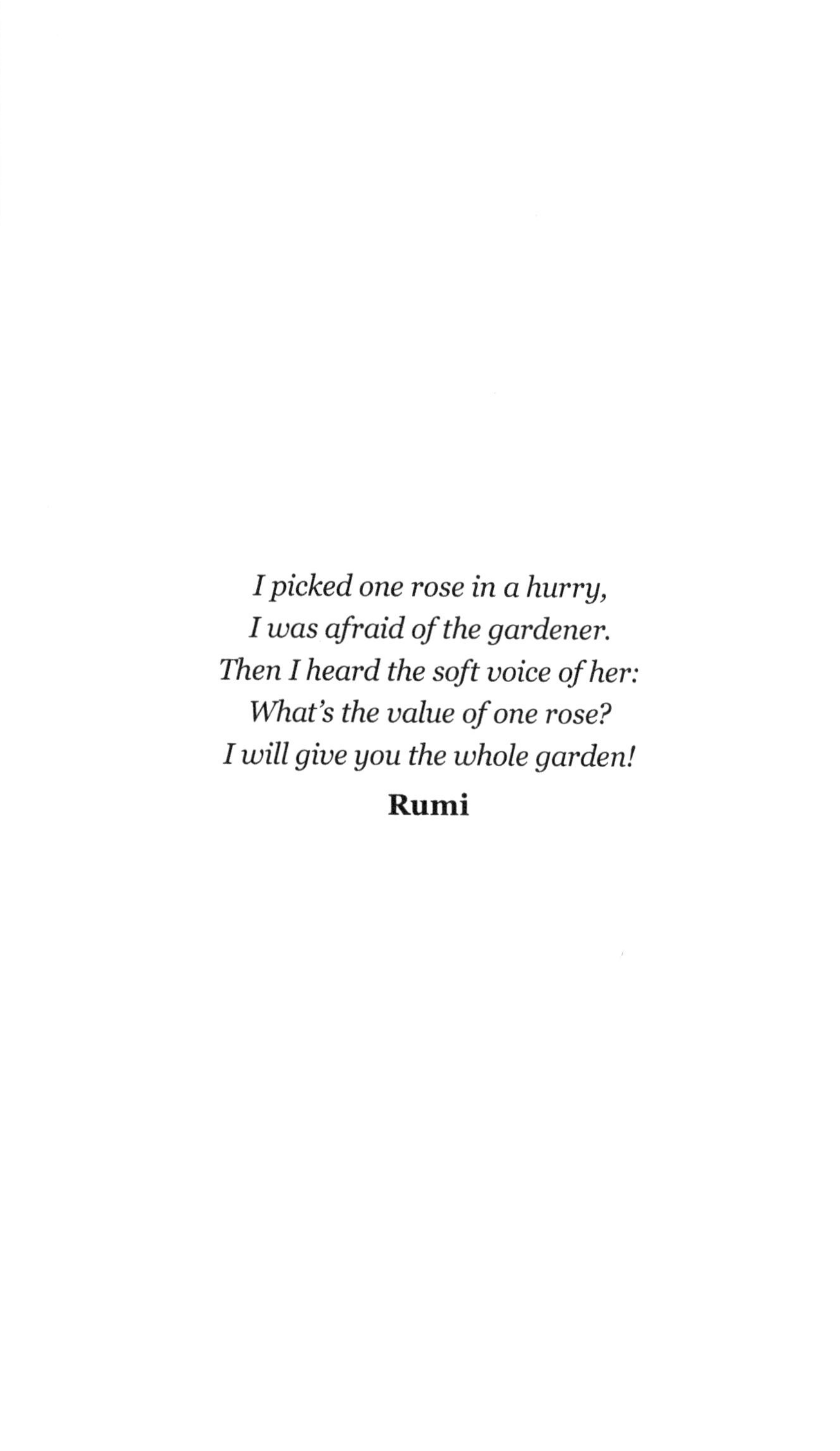

I picked one rose in a hurry,
I was afraid of the gardener.
Then I heard the soft voice of her:
What's the value of one rose?
I will give you the whole garden!

Rumi

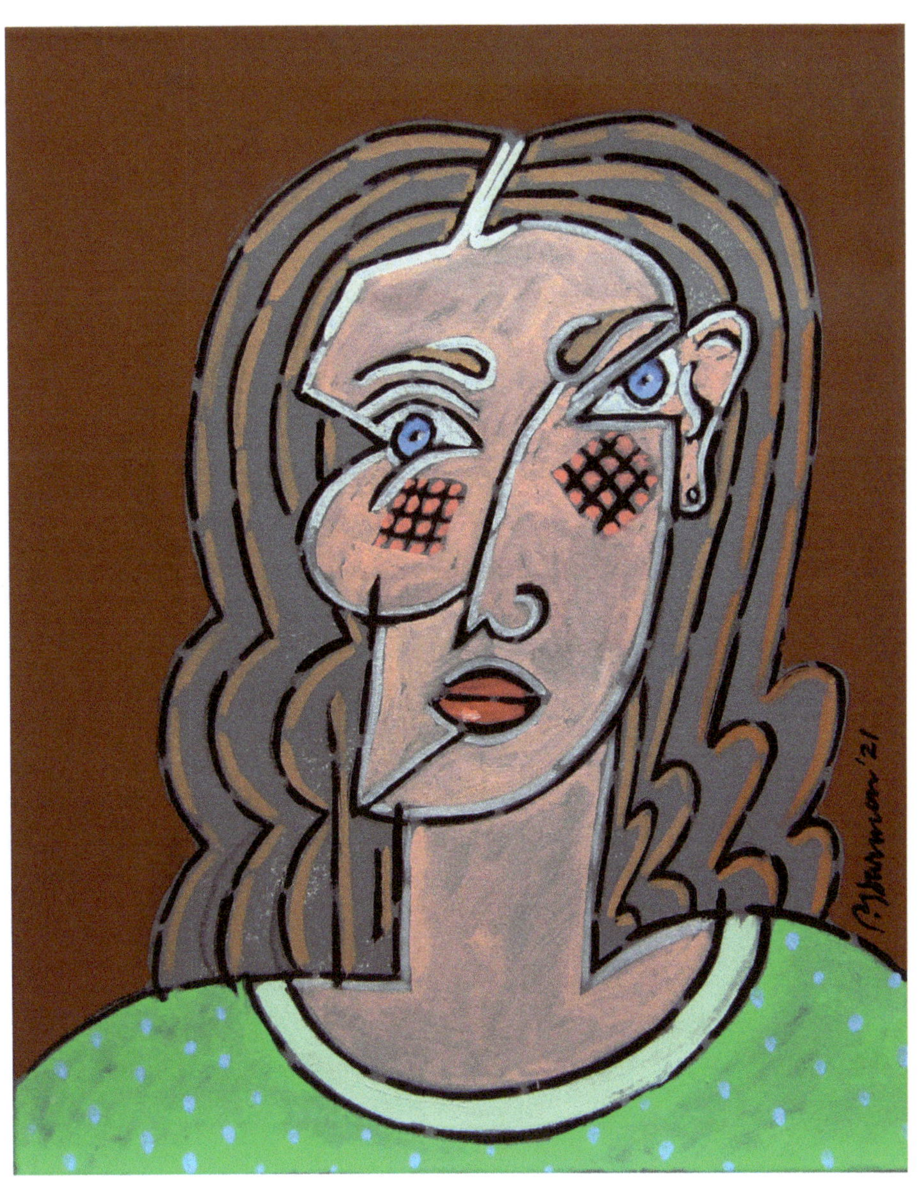

Roll Up Your Sleeves
In This Earthly Dream.
The Buck Starts And Stops With You.
Perceptions Are Clues.
Black And White No Need To Fight.
Insides Pink. Souls Give A Wink.
Heritage Proud. Perceptions Know How.
Choices Drink From An Ancient
Thought Sink.

HTM

Mental associations are living things.
They are formations
Of energy assembled into invisible structures,
Through processes quite as valid
And complicated
As the organization of any group of cells.
Your mental and emotional life

Forms a framework composed of such structures,

And these act directly upon the cells

Of your physical body.

Seth

Jack Rabbit Speed Fear Takes The Lead.
Democracy's Reign Feels The Pain.
Laws Get Trashed. Ignorance Takes Cash.
Capitalists Roam. Freedom's Dethroned.
Inflation Rate. Supply Chain Fate.
Boiling In Angry Stew Is You, Boo.
White Tail Deer Loud And Clear.
Your Angel Spoke And Had A Toke
And Now You're Here.
A Perception Bloke
In Itchy Choices
Covered In
Back Stroke Voices.

HTM

You cannot will yourself to be happy
While believing
You have no right to happiness,
Or you are unworthy of it.
You cannot tell yourself
To release aggressive thoughts
If you think it is wrong
To free them.

Seth

No longer a stranger,
You Listen all day
To these crazy love words.
Like a bee
You fill hundreds of homes with honey,
Though yours
Is a long flight from here.

Rumi

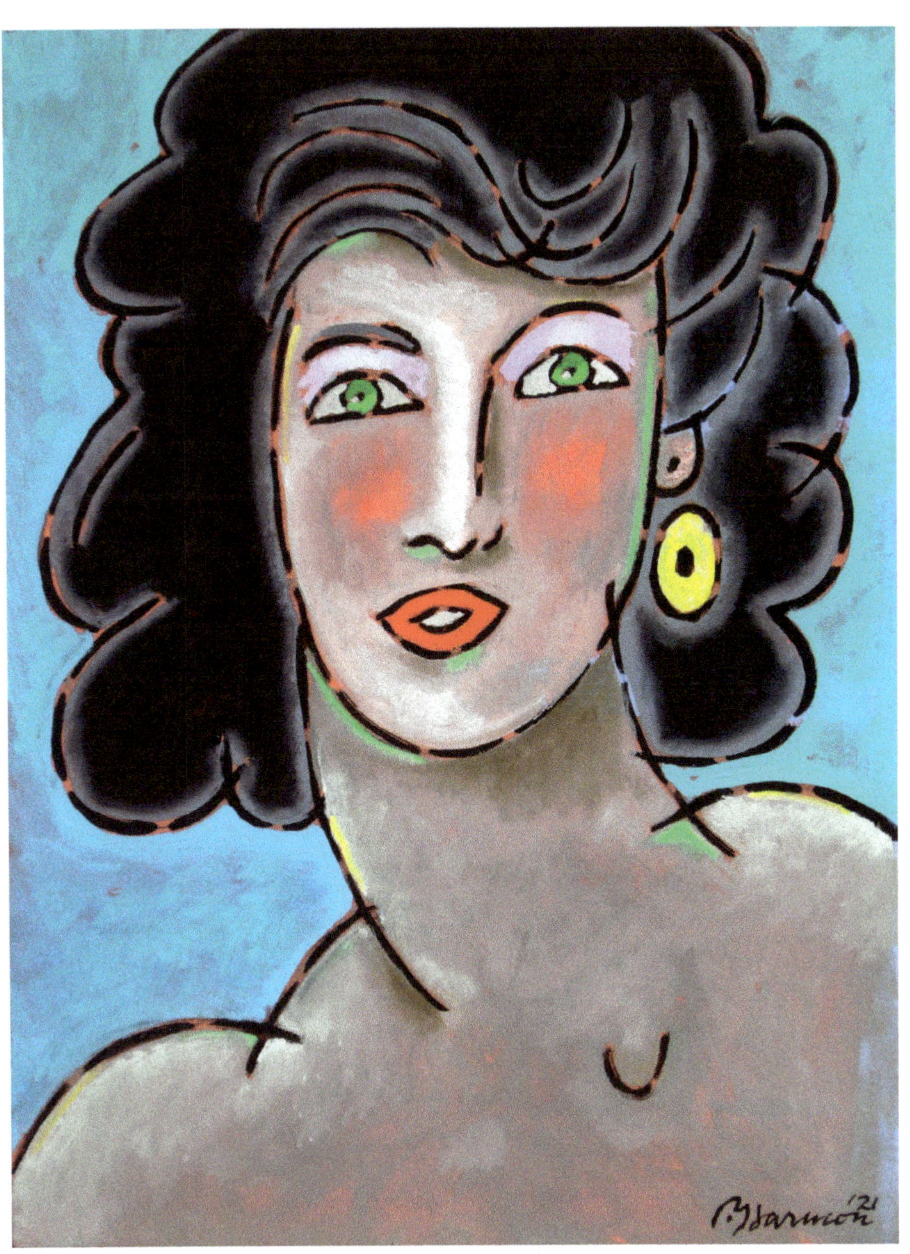

If someone tells you that pleasure is wrong
And tolerance is weakness,
And that you must follow
This or that dogma blindly in obedience,
And that if you are told this is
The only right road toward the idealized good,
Then most likely you are dealing with a fanatic.
If you are told that the end
Justifies any means,
You are dealing with a fanatic.

Seth

Where Is Now
When Clocks Jump Up And Down?
Is It In A Tree Or In Stars?
So Near Yet So Far.
Is It In A Frown?
After An Ego Smack Down?
Or In A Kiss
Before Wedding Bliss?
Or In That Glance
Before Serious Romance?
Is It In War When Emotions Soar?
With Puffs Of Sadness And Bouts Of Madness.
From Thoughts Of Glory
And Old Stories.
While We Swim In Fear
Drinking Beer.

HTM

It's a matter of paying attention to HOW you flow,
And how another individual flows with you
And how YOU flow with them.
Because it's not one way, it's both ways.
And therefore in that,
It's a matter of recognizing
That it's not only how the other individual flows with you
Or complements you,
But how do you complement them also?

Seth

Inherent in practically all artists' work
Is a desire to talk to you.
But everyone is not comfortable
And familiar with the language
We Artists use.
Using line and color we talk with a language
That has developed over a period
Of some thirty-five thousand years
And includes a lot of abbreviations,
Symbols, shorthand, as well as
Some Invented language
That even we don't understand yet.
The puzzle can be mysterious and intimidating.
But it's not math. It's not science.
There is no right or wrong.

Paul Harmon

This aloneness
Is worth more than a thousand lives.
This freedom is worth more
Than all the lands on earth.
To be one with the truth
For just a moment,
Is worth more than the world
And life itself.

Rumi

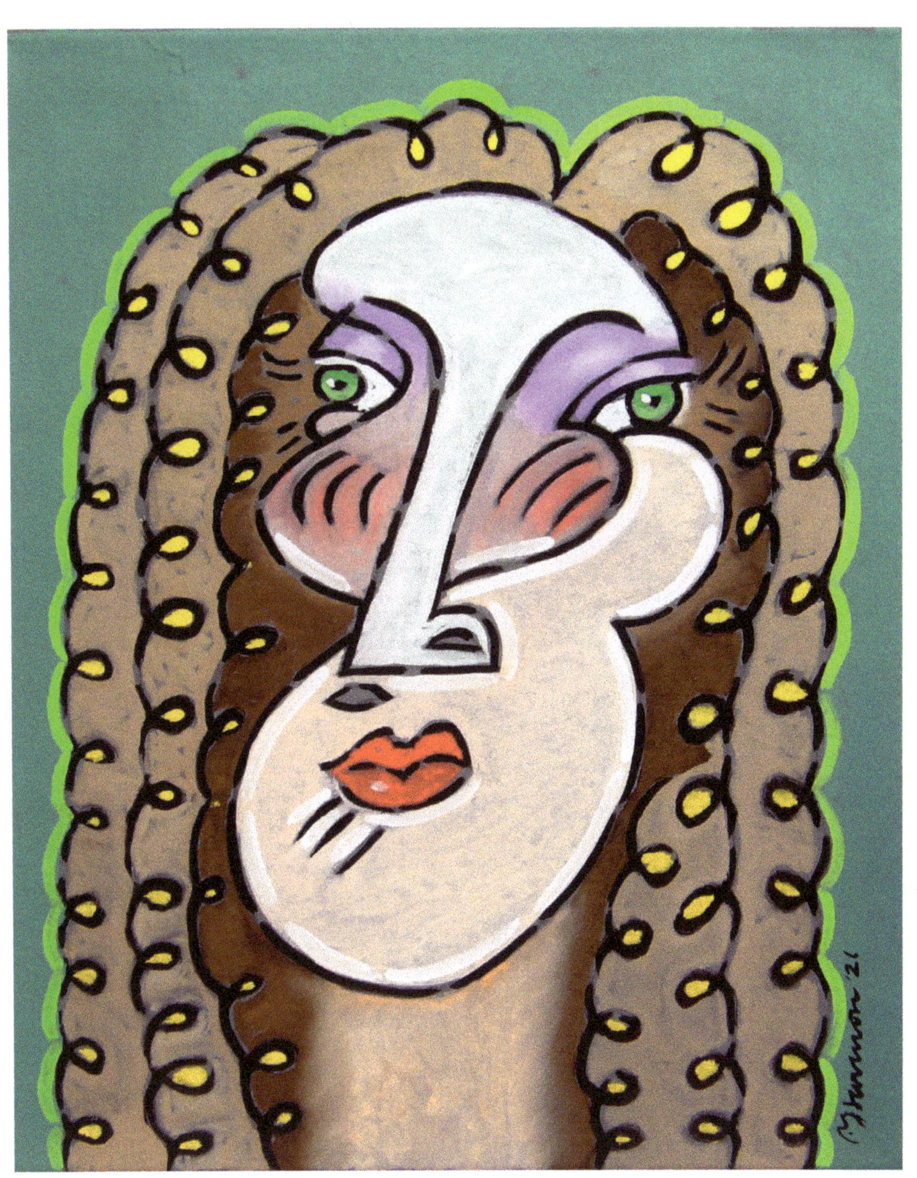

Bottomless Pit In The Land Of The Rich.
Anything Goes.
As Long As The Money Flows.
Dirty Socks. Crusades For Mops.
Religion For Grins. Justice Never Wins.
There's No Place In An Ego Rat Race
But At The Top.
The Rest Is Slop.
But Stop That Band.
That Ain't Music Man.
Perceptions Block The Lock
That Free Beliefs Tattered Flock.
Like Roasted Flies
In A Light Bulb Fry.
Wilted Bees. Guns Hanging Trees
Waiting For A Chance
To Stick Choices
In Your Pants.

HTM

Once you understand the symbolic nature of physical reality,
Then you will no longer feel entrapped by it.
You have formed the symbols,
And therefore you can change them.
You must learn, of course,
What the various symbols mean in your own life,
And how to translate their meaning.

Seth

Mind Your Manners In All The Clamor.
Hidden Fears. Nerves Have Ears.
Cells Explode When Thoughts Erode.
Redwood Stumps. Tornado Thumps.
Earth's Magnetic Ball Needs An Overhaul.
Silver Binding. Anger's Climbing.
Choices Hit The Ground
Like A Sack Of Egos
In Lost And Found.
While Time Throws Life Down
In Thoughts That Add A Pound
Of Anxiety In Every Sound.

HTM

For a long time,
I have been guided
Internally by an embracing view
Of this thing called making art.
It didn't hurt Picasso and Matisse
And many others to claim
Cezanne (as an example)
As their spiritual grandfather.
He didn't have to be killed off
So they could create
A new art beyond him.

Paul Harmon

My poems resemble the bread of Egypt...
One night passes over it,
And you can't eat it anymore.
So gobble them down now,
While they're still fresh,
Before the dust of the worlds settles on them.
Where a poem belongs is here,
In the warmth of the chest;
Out in the world it dies of cold.

Rumi

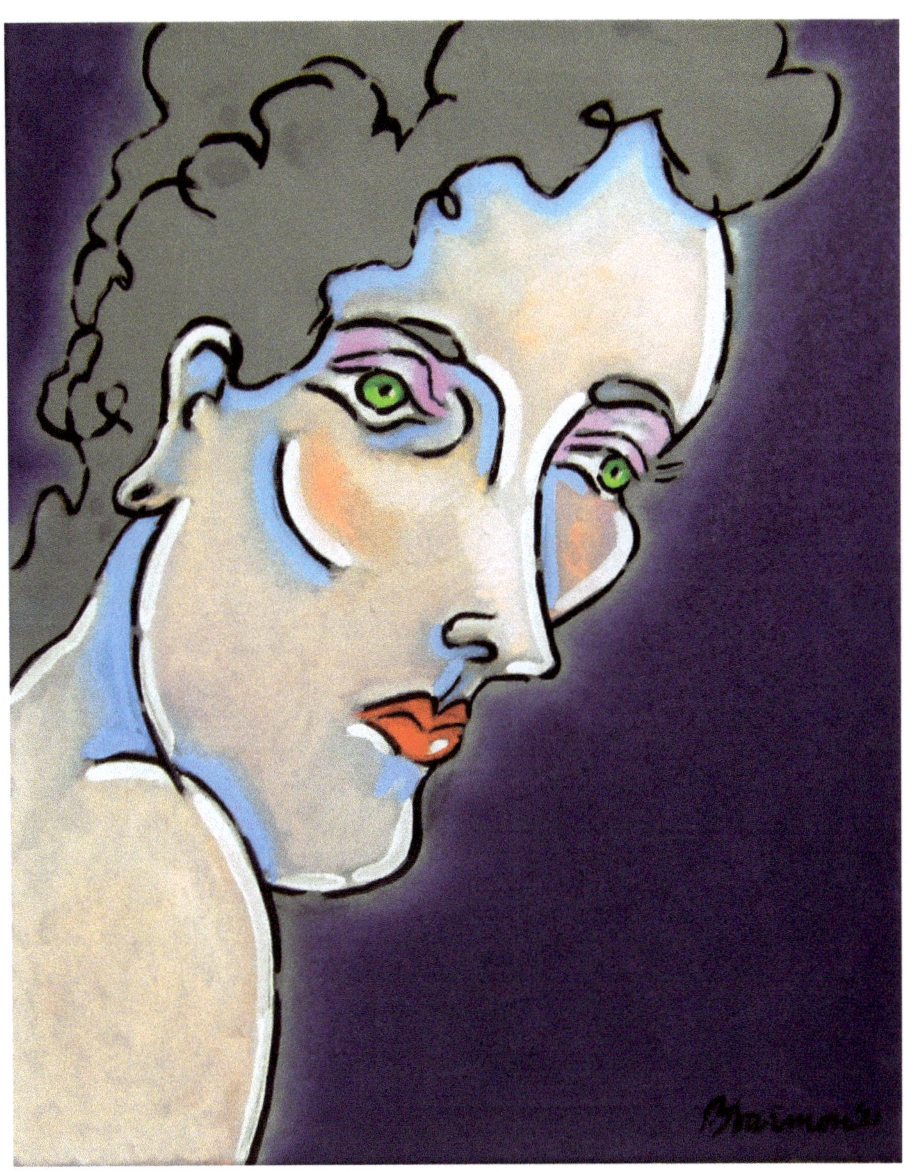

When I speak of the whole self
I am of course referring to the personality
As it exists in its entirety,
Having at its command
Use of both the inner and outer senses.
That is, I speak of the doer,
The mover, the breather
And the dreamer
As all belonging
To one whole self.

Seth

Even though I have surrendered
To my natural instincts,
I find that I have followed
A clear and straight path.
Along the way,
There have been great fogs,
But when they have cleared,
I found that I had not veered
Off the path.
This is astonishing to me.
What exactly was I using
As a compass?

Paul Harmon

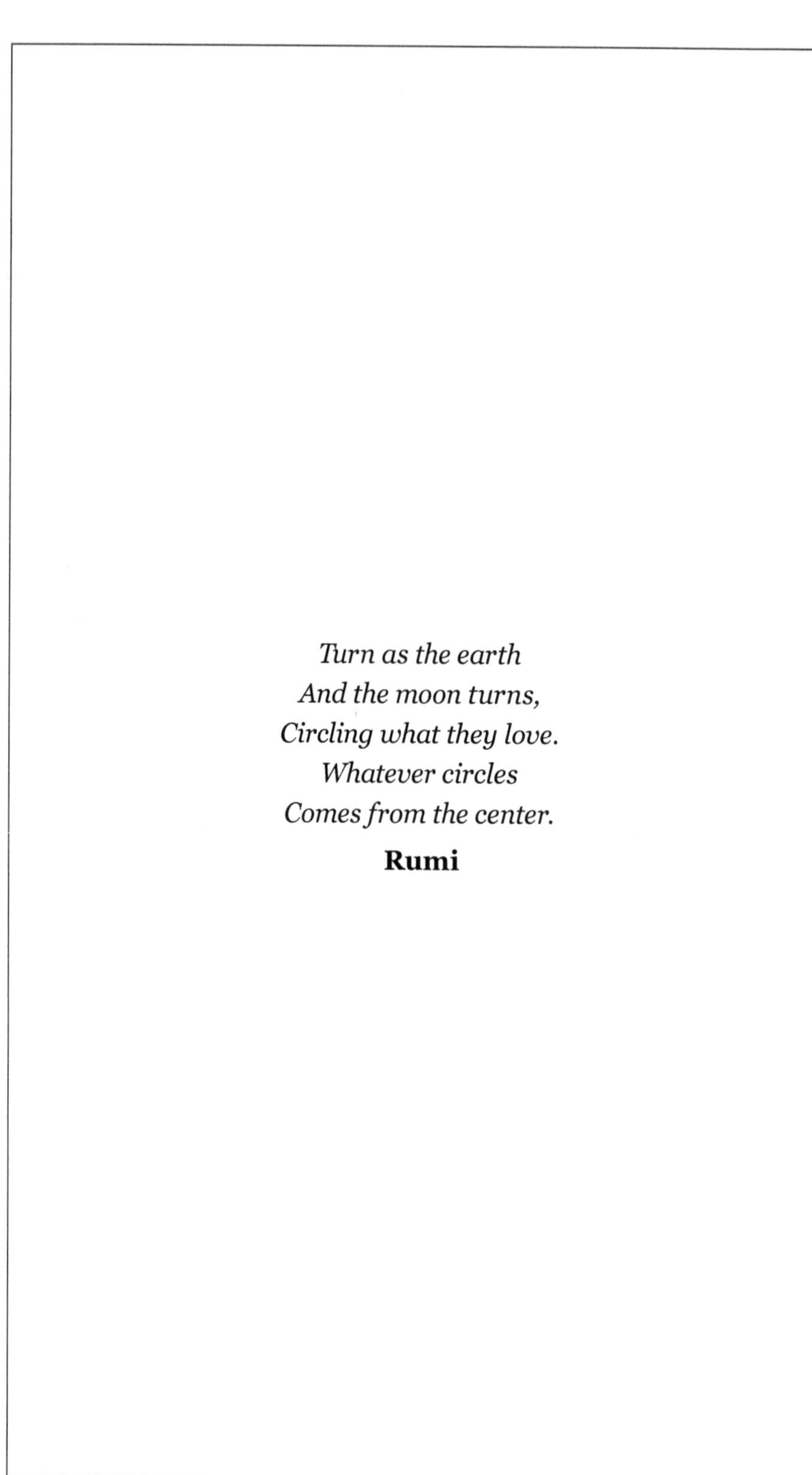

Turn as the earth
And the moon turns,
Circling what they love.
Whatever circles
Comes from the center.

Rumi

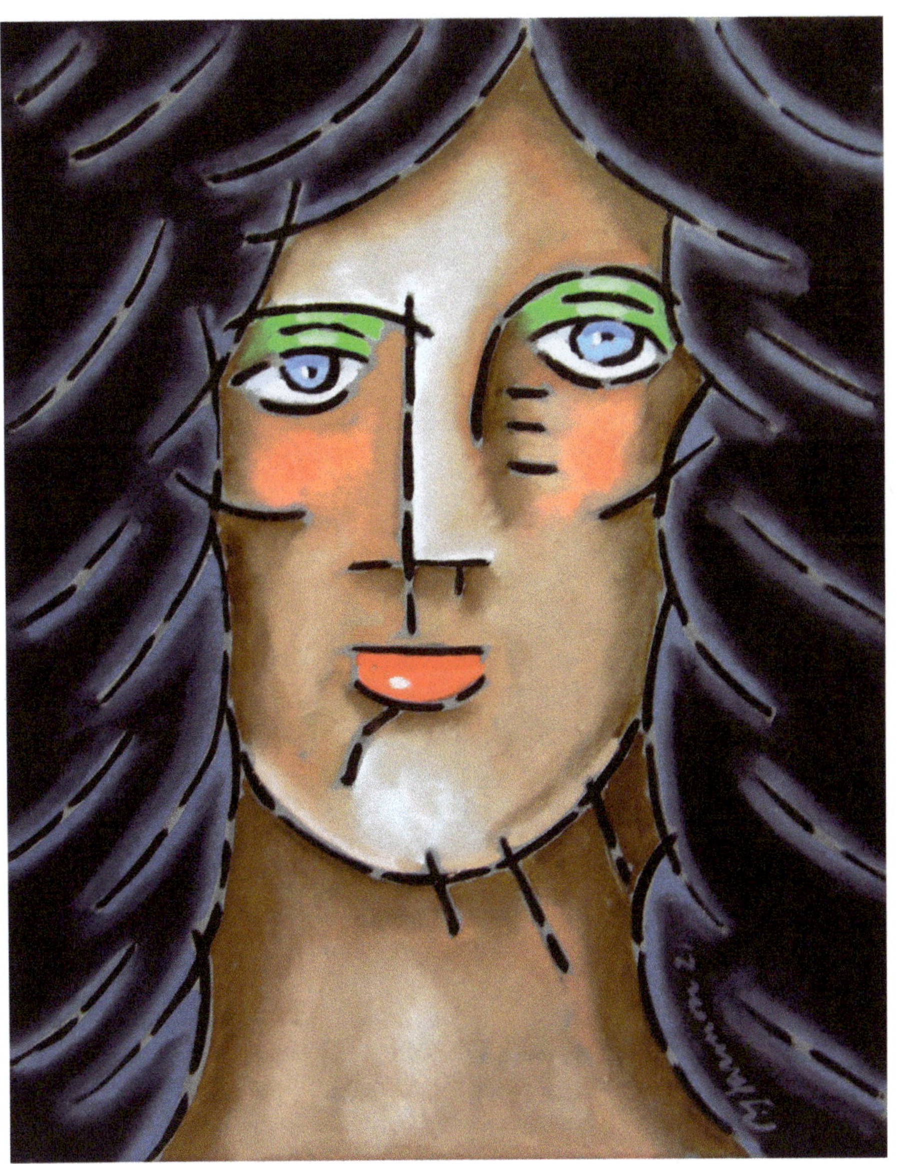

About The Author

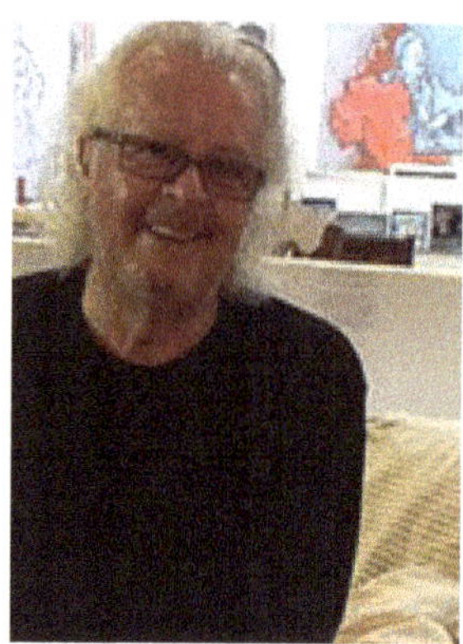

There's no denying it. My physical personality was lost in one crazy bad-ass netherworld of misremembering for the first forty-seven years of my life. My inner personality kept getting body-slammed by my physical one while I built my egocentric world. I like to say I was a religious, capitalistic slave, immersed in a vat of distorted values. And here's the thing: that is a realistic description of the physical image I created through years of business conditioning and knee-jerk personal choices.

I was a hardheaded, egotistical college dropout with doctoral-level personality skills. My goal was to sell my way to fame and glory, one shoe at a time. I was a money-hungry young shoe salesman—a shoe salesman willing to do the low-class ego dance for an order. I had the capitalistic brazenness to move up the corporate shoe ladder.

My capitalistic persona would always stretch reason-ability to its outer limits. So when I failed a time or two or three, I blamed the system. But I rose from my self-created ashes and got objectively successful again by selling more than one shoe at a time. I was selling container loads of shoes at one time. And once I felt successful, I wanted more power and more recognition.

When I bet it all with a blundering, alcohol-enriched mind I offered my impressive shoe talents to the capitalistic wolves, expecting to become one. But my narrow-minded focus sent me over the cliff of self-discovery. My physical personality was in free fall, and all my lifelines burned in a fire I made. My reality started to change, and I started to feel another presence within me. My inner personality guided me to the bottom, so I could internally heal my self-imposed wounds.

Once I hit bottom, my physical personality drifted in a mysterious mixture of self-pity and irrelevance. But my inner personality came to the rescue. The energy within my inner personality took over when my mother passed in 1996. And that personality helped me understand the passing of my younger brother, Bob, and my dad, Howard, in 2013. I felt something special during these monumental losses. It felt like I was standing in a nonphysical stream of understanding, and I felt the pure energy in that understanding.

My physical personality followed that stream when I began reading psychology and philosophy books. I found Rumi quotes in many of those books, so at forty-seven, I bought my first book of poetry. The Essential Rumi by Coleman Barks introduced me to some of his thoughts. Rumi, the thirteenth-century Sufi mystic, is an inner-self shaker. I started to look at the nonphysical part of things because of Rumi.

Then Confucius, Lao Tzu, Buddha, the German poet Rainer Maria Rilke, and the Englishman William Blake gave me their versions of inner personality expressions. Jesus, Muhammad, Ralph Waldo Emerson, Ernest Holmes, James Allen, and other soul-seekers through the ages all said the same thing. And they all used their inner personalities to say it.

By the time I found Japan's Shinkichi Takahashi's work, I was on the edge of a nonphysical bridge. I realized that I'd been on that bridge all my physical life but ignored being there. I'd always felt the presence of an agreeable being in my thoughts. But I rarely paid attention to that being until I read *Ask and It Is Given* as soon as it hit the bookstores.

Abraham, the author of the book, is a nonphysical energy personality who expresses commonsense thoughts about the nature of physical life.

Then I hit the jackpot when I found the *Seth Material.* Jane Roberts, the poet and writer, brought the thoughts of nonphysical Seth into my world during my fifties. When Elias and Zurac came into my life in the first decade of the twenty-first century through the internet and a booth at Nashville's Galactic Expo, I realized that these nonphysical personalities' unfiltered messages were helping me forge an unfiltered path on this physical journey.

What I've learned on this journey is that I am here to physically experience my thoughts, emotions, perceptions, and choices. I know now what the sages and the people who used their inner senses in this reality were trying to tell me and everyone else: *Our thoughts and emotions are forms of energy that act like cells when we project them into our reality using a mechanism we call "perception."* They are the tools we use to create what we experience physically.

I'm not here to form a group or write sermons about self-responsibility. And I'm not here to act like someone who crossed the self-awareness finish line and is basking in a state of bliss. My physical personality is still physically focused on creating my reality. But I'm increasingly using my inner personality to do it. I live in more than one reality. And I'm just beginning to appreciate what these other realities do for me.

READER VIEWS LITERARY AWARDS WINNER - THE LAWN PARTY AND EVERYONE'S INVITED

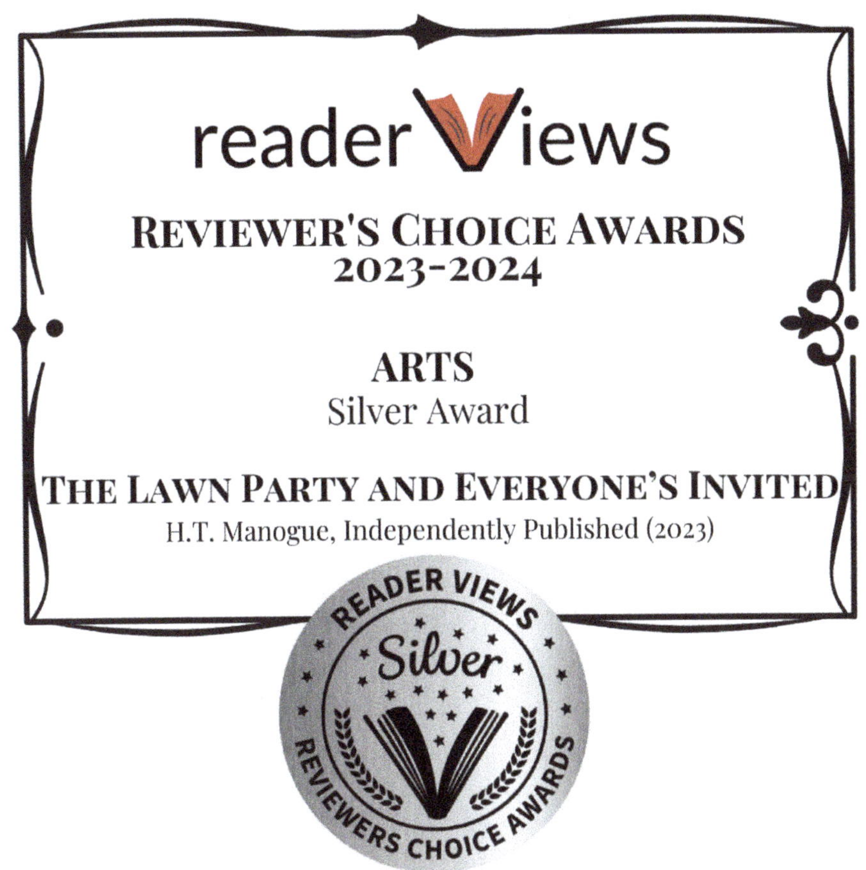

It is with immense pleasure that we extend our heartfelt congratulations on being one of the esteemed winners of the 2023-2024 Reader Views Literary Awards program. This achievement is a testament to your extraordinary talent and the innovative spirit you bring to the world of literature, especially within the vibrant community of self-published authors.

www.ingramcontent.com/pod-product-compliance
Lightning Source LLC
LaVergne TN
LVHW051939100826
845155LV00006B/18
9798218137007